SHEaR DEVOTIONAL DELIGHT

(Nourishing Devotions for Healthy Sheep)

Drs. Don and Debbi Dunlap

Lulu Publishing, Inc.

Morrisville, NC

SHEaR DEVOTIONAL DELIGHT
(Nourishing Devotions for Healthy Sheep)
Published by Lulu Publishers, Inc.
3131 RDU Center, Suite 210
Morrisville, NC 27560

Copyright ©2005 Don Dunlap. All rights reserved. Without the prior permission of the authors, no portion of this book may be reproduced other than the study guide at the end.

Printed in the United States of America

ISBN 1-4116-2881-0

All Scripture references are used by permission and are from the New American Standard Bible, used by permission, copyright ©The Lockman Foundation, 1960, 1962, 1963, 1968, 1971, 1972, 1973, 1975, 1977, and the King James Version.

Foreword

Don't you just love the idea of being a sheep in God's fold? Reading books on topics like conflict resolution, anger management, or child discipline will undoubtedly improve the quality of your life.

But until you begin spending regular time alone with the Good Shepherd, you won't experience substantive growth in your Christian journey.

A quick look in the religious section of any bookstore will yield a wide variety of devotional books to choose from—from the more lightweight, inspirational types, to timeless classics by such greats as Oswald Chambers and Charles H. Spurgeon.

This little book is a compilation of various devotionals we've written through the years, primarily to teach Believers the rich themes of the Christian faith, such as God's purpose in suffering, running the good race, loving enemies, the importance of forgiveness, denying self, demonstrating a servant's heart, our significance in Christ, the nobility of labor, the difference between thanking God and praising Him, obeying authorities, and understanding God's holiness.

You'll note that these selections, each one drawn directly from God's Word, are not written in the anecdotal style of most present-day devotional books. So, dear fellow sheep, with no further "baa-nter," we pray you'll find "shear" delight and genuine encouragement in the pages that follow.

-Don and Debbi Dunlap

Personal Devotions

One of the most exciting truths of the Christian life is this: We are His people and the sheep of His pasture. He is our loving, faithful Shepherd who tenderly cares for us. According to John 10:11, He is the *Good* Shepherd—One who lays down His life for His sheep.

A healthy sheep is a happy sheep. If *you* are one of His sheep, you need to be led by still waters—every day. And you need to be made to lie down in green pastures—every day. Why is this true? Well, let's break it down to basics.

First, sheep need to be led, because they can't get there on their own. Left to their own resources and devices, they're not-so-smart sheep—fallen from God's grace and terribly marred by sin. "Bent creatures," to borrow C.S. Lewis' poignant description.

Second, sheep have to drink water every day to avoid dehydration and continue existing. Our Shepherd is the Living Water who thoroughly satisfies His sheep, unlike any other can ever satisfy.

Third, sheep need to be made to rest in green pastures. Otherwise, they will die of exhaustion. Our Shepherd is the One in whom we live, move, and find our rest. We can rest peacefully and confidently in Him because He is Truth, He is wholly trustworthy, and He knows every sheep's life in mind-boggling detail. And He still loves us.

Fourth, sheep must be coaxed to graze in plush, verdant meadows for their sustenance, lest they starve to death. Our Shepherd is the Bread of Life who fills the deepest hunger of every sheep's heart.

We mustn't overlook this final important point: sheep need loving discipline. They are full of mischief, and concerned, first and foremost, with their own selfish needs. Without the Good Shepherd's rod of chastisement, sheep would quickly lead themselves into deadly situations.

Consider our Shepherd's words in John 10:27,28: "My sheep hear My voice and they follow Me, and I give eternal life to them. They shall never perish and no one shall snatch them out of My hand."

Sheep need to spend consistent time with the Good Shepherd on a regular basis. Some refer to this as daily devotions; others call it a quiet time.

We prefer the term "Private Devotions." Of course, the important thing isn't what you call it, but just to meet with the Lord each day and spend concentrated time in His presence, praising Him, thanking Him, reading Scripture, praying, listening to Him, and seeking His face.

Certainly, there's no *one* way to meet with God each day. But we are convinced there *are* a few tips for having a more quality experience with Him during your private devotional time.

If you've never been taught *how* to spend maximum time in personal devotions with the Lord, or if you'd simply like to have more meaningful meetings alone with God, we urge you to consider some of the following suggestions.

Try to find some special place where you can meet with the Lord every day. Then decide when you will schedule your daily meeting with Him. Some people discover that the best time for private devotions is in the evening.

In the book of Genesis, God says, "The evening and the morning were the first day." So there's a valid basis for scheduling personal devotions in the evening—to set your heart for the night's rest, and for the work and activities awaiting you the following day.

Others find that early in the morning is the quietest time of day for them, before the many demands of life begin to vie for their attention.

Besides your Bible, a notebook and pen, you may need a hymnal, praise and worship choruses, a CD player or tape player, etc. It's helpful to keep all the materials you use for your private devotions stored in a desk or table, for example, at your "meeting place" so you don't waste valuable time each day searching for them.

==Remember that this is the single most important meeting of your day. Guard this time carefully. It is a divine appointment with your Savior.== Don't allow interruptions to distract you from your commitment to spend time alone with God.

Renowned Christian leader George Mueller, (who prayed many orphanages into existence in England in the 1800's, without ever asking anyone for money, and telling his needs to God alone), offers this excellent advice regarding private devotions: *"The key to successful living is daily to seek God's face before you greet the face of man, and daily to listen to God's voice before you hear the voice of man."*

Here are some further suggestions:

1. ***Start by praising God.***

    Think about "entering His gates with thanksgiving in your heart, and entering His courts with praise." Sing hymns and praise choruses aloud to the Lord. Praise Him for His holy character and attributes such as faithfulness, justice, mercy, goodness, and forgiveness. During this time, concentrate on exalting Him with a grateful heart. Don't ask Him for anything.

2. **Go to God's Word.**

    Read Scripture, or listen to the Bible on CD or cassette. A good idea is to listen to the Bible while you get in your daily walk or exercise. If you'd like to read through the Bible in one year, use the suggested plan included a little later in this chapter.

3. **Reading a devotional book is recommended.**

    Morning and Evening, by C.H. Spurgeon, and *Keep a Quiet Heart*, by Elisabeth Elliot are both exceptional devotional books that stand out among the many excellent ones available on the market. (It takes about 5 minutes to read each selection.)

4. **Spend time praying.**

    Before you begin a time of concentrated prayer, use this helpful checklist to get your heart and mind prepared:

    Are You Ready to Pray?

❑ **Are all sins confessed?**

"If we say that we have not sinned, we make Him a liar and His Word is not in us." 1 John 1:10

- ❏ **Are all relationships with others made right?**

We should never come before God to worship Him or to pray to Him if we know we have unresolved conflict with someone.

As far as it is possible with us, we should first make every effort to reconcile a broken relationship. Only then can we come before the Lord with "clean hands and a pure heart," as described in the Psalms.

"For if you forgive men for their transgressions, your heavenly Father will also forgive you. But if you do not forgive men, then your Father will not forgive your transgressions." Matthew 6:24,25

- ❏ **Are you seeking His will in all things?**

You should be ready to accept a "no" from God as readily as you'd accept a "yes." He may even answer with a "wait." But that should also be agreeable to you if you truly want to know and do His will more than you want your own way in a particular situation or circumstance. Submit your will to His.

"And this is the confidence which we have before Him, that if we ask anything according to His will, He hears us. And if we know that He hears us in whatever we ask, we know that we have the requests which we have asked from Him." 1 John 5:14,15

❏ **Are you seeking to glorify God above all things?**

Are you asking God to make a certain thing come to pass in your life, because it would make you happy, or it would make your life easier?

Well, those certainly aren't bad reasons to pray, but they're not the reason we *should* pray, and they're definitely not the *best* motivation for prayer.
We ought to have a burning desire to bring glory to God. To honor Him above all else. So we ask Him to answer our prayers in such a way that will glorify Himself, whether the answer suits us personally or not.

"And whatever you ask in My name, that will I do, that the Father may be glorified in the Son. If you ask Me anything in My name, I will do it." John 14:13, 14

❏ **Are you depending on the Holy Spirit's guidance?**

"And in the same way, the Spirit also helps our weakness, for we do not know how to pray as we should, but the Spirit Himself intercedes for us with groaning too deep for words; and He who searches the hearts knows what the mind of the Spirit is, because He intercedes for the saints according to the will of God." Romans 8:26, 27

❏ **Are you trusting God in spite of what "seems" to be?**

"Trust in the Lord with all your heart, and do not lean on your own understanding. In all your ways acknowledge Him, and He will make your paths straight." Proverbs 3:5,6

❑ **Will you praise God no matter what?**

"And we know that God causes all things to work together for good to those who love God, to those who are called according to His purpose." Romans 8:28

"ACTS" is a helpful acrostic for remembering the scriptural basis for prayer:

A – Adoration: *"Enter His gates with thanksgiving and His courts with praise." Psalm 100:4*

- Contemplate the glorious nature of God. Begin your time of prayer by thanking God for His attributes, such as His goodness, mercy, power, faithfulness, holiness, and wisdom.

- Thank Him for Who He is, rather than for what He does for you. This is pleasing to God, and demonstrates that you are not approaching Him with your hand out, asking Him to do something for you. It expresses the fact that if He never did another thing for you, you would love Him for His perfect character.

C – Confession: *"If we confess our sins, He is faithful and just to forgive us our sins and to cleanse us from all unrighteousness." 1 John 1:9*

- In a spirit of honest self-examination, ask the Holy Spirit to shine a searchlight on your heart.

Humble yourself before God and invite Him to penetrate the depths of your being and reveal to you any sins that reside within.

- Make of list of the things God brings to your mind and heart. Repent of each sin, specifically, and confess each one to the Lord, asking for forgiveness, and thanking Him for cleansing you as He promised.

T – Thanksgiving: *"In everything give thanks, for this is the will of God in Christ concerning you."*
1 Thessalonians 5:18

- Ingratitude is one of our most grievous sins. Purpose to be like the one leper Jesus healed who returned to express his thanks to Christ.

- Count your blessings, naming them specifically. Remember the mighty, wondrous things God has done for you.

S – Supplication: *"If you abide in Me and My words abide in you, ask what you will and it shall be done unto you." John 15:7*

- In faith, believing that God hears your prayers, make your requests and petitions known before His throne—your own needs and prayers for others.

- Don't be double-minded, but boldly approach His throne to find help in time of need. It has been noted that we are most like Jesus when we intercede (pray) for others.

Journaling

- We recommend you keep a notebook and pen handy to record insights from Scripture as you spend time in the Word.

- Divide your notebook in half. In the second section, log your prayer requests and God's answers. This helps you *"forget not the benefits of the Lord."* It also becomes a record of God's faithfulness in your life to hand down to your children and your grandchildren.

There are several good "Read through the Bible" plans you can use. We happen to like the one we've provided in this chapter, because it allows for reading from the Old and New Testaments nearly every day.

Does the thought of reading through the whole Bible seem overwhelming to you? The encouraging news is, if you only read about 3 ½ chapters a day, you can read through the entire 1,189 chapters of the Bible in one year—929 Old Testament chapters and 260 New Testament chapters in the New Testament. You'll read from the Psalms every tenth day.

And don't worry—most everyone gets behind sometimes in a plan like this. Just set aside one day a month for catch-up. The wisdom and godly knowledge you'll glean from faithfully and consistently reading God's Word, is worth every bit of the effort you'll make to stick with the reading schedule.

Check the box by each daily Bible reading selection when you complete it. Remember to jot down insights in your journal.

January

- [ ] 1. **Genesis 1-4**
- [ ] 2. **Genesis 5-8**
- [ ] 3. **Genesis 9-11**
- [ ] 4. **Genesis 12-15**
- [ ] 5. **Genesis 16-19**
- [ ] 6. **Genesis 20-23**
- [ ] 7. **Genesis 24-26**
- [ ] 8. **Genesis 27-30**
- [ ] 9. **Genesis 31-33**
- [ ] 10. **Genesis 34-37**
- [ ] 11. **Genesis 38-41**
- [ ] 12. **Genesis 42-44**
- [ ] 13. **Genesis 45-47**
- [ ] 14. **Genesis 48-50**
- [ ] 15. **Psalms 1-4**
- [ ] 16. **Psalms 5-8**
- [ ] 17. **Exodus 1-4**
- [ ] 18. **Exodus 5-7**
- [ ] 19. **Exodus 8-10**
- [ ] 20. **Exodus 11-13**
- [ ] 21. **Exodus 14-16**
- [ ] 22. **Exodus 17-19**
- [ ] 23. **Exodus 20-22**
- [ ] 24. **Psalms 9-12**

- ☐ 25. **Exodus 23-25**
- ☐ 26. **Exodus 26-28**
- ☐ 27. **Exodus 27-31**
- ☐ 28. **Exodus 32-34**
- ☐ 29. **Exodus 35-37**
- ☐ 30. **Exodus 38-40**
- ☐ 31. **Leviticus 1-4**

February

- ☐ 1. **Leviticus 5-8**
- ☐ 2. **Psalms 13-16**
- ☐ 3. **Leviticus 9-12** & **John 1**
- ☐ 4. **Leviticus 13-15** & **John 2**
- ☐ 5. **Leviticus 16-18** & **John 3**
- ☐ 6. **Leviticus 19-21** & **John 4**
- ☐ 7. **Leviticus 22-24** & **John 5**
- ☐ 8. **Leviticus 25-27** & **John 6**
- ☐ 9. **Numbers 1-2** & **John 7**
- ☐ 10. **Numbers 3-4** & **John 8**
- ☐ 11. **Psalms 17-20**
- ☐ 12. **Numbers 5-6** & **John 9**
- ☐ 13. **Numbers 7-8** & **John 10**
- ☐ 14. **Numbers 9-10** & **John 11**
- ☐ 15. **Numbers 11-12** & **John 12**
- ☐ 16. **Numbers 13-14** & **John 13**
- ☐ 17. **Numbers 15-16** & **John 14**
- ☐ 18. **Numbers 17-18** & **John 15**
- ☐ 19. **Numbers 19-20** & **John 16**

- [ ] 20. **Psalms 21-24**
- [ ] 21. **Numbers 21-22** & **John 17**
- [ ] 22. **Numbers 23-24** & **John 18**
- [ ] 23. **Numbers 25-26** & **John 19**
- [ ] 24. **Numbers 27-28** & **John 20**
- [ ] 25. **Numbers 29-30** & **John 21**
- [ ] 26. **Numbers 31-32**
- [ ] 27. **Numbers 33-34**
- [ ] 28. **Numbers 35-36**

March

- [ ] 1. **Psalms 25-28**
- [ ] 2. **Deuteronomy 1-2** & **Matthew 1**
- [ ] 3. **Deuteronomy 3-4** & **Matthew 2**
- [ ] 4. **Deuteronomy 5-6** & **Matthew 3**
- [ ] 5. **Deuteronomy 7-8**
- [ ] 6. **Deuteronomy 9-10** & **Matthew 4**
- [ ] 7. **Deuteronomy 11-12**
- [ ] 8. **Deuteronomy 13-14** & **Matthew 5**
- [ ] 9. **Deuteronomy 15-16**
- [ ] 10. **Psalms 29-32**
- [ ] 11. **Deuteronomy 17-18** & **Matthew 6**
- [ ] 12. **Deuteronomy 19-20**
- [ ] 13. **Deuteronomy 21-22** & **Matthew 7**
- [ ] 14. **Deuteronomy 23-24**
- [ ] 15. **Deuteronomy 25-26** & **Matthew 8**
- [ ] 16. **Deuteronomy 27-28**
- [ ] 17. **Deuteronomy 29-30** & **Matthew 9**

- ☐ 18. **Deuteronomy 31-32**
- ☐ 19. **Deuteronomy 33-34 & Matthew 10**
- ☐ 20. **Psalms 33-36**
- ☐ 21. **Joshua 1-2 & Matthew 11**
- ☐ 22. **Joshua 3-4**
- ☐ 23. **Joshua 5-6 & Matthew 12**
- ☐ 24. **Joshua 7-8**
- ☐ 25. **Joshua 9-10 & Matthew 13**
- ☐ 26. **Joshua 11-12**
- ☐ 27. **Joshua 13-14 & Matthew 14**
- ☐ 28. **Psalms 37-40**
- ☐ 29. **Joshua 15-16 & Matthew 15**
- ☐ 30. **Joshua 17-18**
- ☐ 31. **Joshua 19-20** & **Matthew 16**

April

- ☐ 1. **Joshua 21-22**
- ☐ 2. **Joshua 23-24 & Matthew 17**
- ☐ 3. **Judges 1-2**
- ☐ 4. **Judges 3-4 & Matthew 18**
- ☐ 5. **Judges 5-6**
- ☐ 6. **Psalms 41-44**
- ☐ 7. **Judges 7-8 & Matthew 19**
- ☐ 8. **Judges 9-10**
- ☐ 9. **Judges 11-12 & Matthew 20**
- ☐ 10. **Judges 13-14**
- ☐ 11. **Judges 15-16 & Matthew 21**
- ☐ 12. **Judges 17-18**

- ☐ 13. **Judges 19-21**
- ☐ 14. **Ruth 1-4**
- ☐ 15. **Psalms 45-48**
- ☐ 16. **1 Samuel 1-2 & Matthew 22**
- ☐ 17. **1 Samuel 3-4**
- ☐ 18. **1 Samuel 5-6 & Matthew 23**
- ☐ 19. **1 Samuel 7-8**
- ☐ 20. **1 Samuel 9-10 & Matthew 24**
- ☐ 21. **1 Samuel 11-12**
- ☐ 22. **1 Samuel 13-14**
- ☐ 23. **1 Samuel 15-16 & Matthew 25**
- ☐ 24. **Psalms 49-52**
- ☐ 25. **1 Samuel 17-18 & Matthew 26**
- ☐ 26. **1 Samuel 19-20**
- ☐ 27. **1 Samuel 21-22 & Matthew 27**
- ☐ 28. **1 Samuel 23-24**
- ☐ 29. **1 Samuel 25-26**
- ☐ 30. **1 Samuel 27-28** & **Matthew 28**

May

- ☐ 1. **1 Samuel 29-31**
- ☐ 2. **Psalms 53-56**
- ☐ 3. **2 Samuel 1-2 & Mark 1**
- ☐ 4. **2 Samuel 3-4**
- ☐ 5. **2 Samuel 5-6 & Mark 2**
- ☐ 6. **2 Samuel 7-8**
- ☐ 7. **2 Samuel 9-10 & Mark 3**
- ☐ 8. **2 Samuel 11-12**

- [ ] 9. **2 Samuel 13-14** & **Mark 4**
- [ ] 10. **2 Samuel 15-16**
- [ ] 11. **2 Samuel 17-18**
- [ ] 12. **Psalms 57-60**
- [ ] 13. **2 Samuel 19-20** & **Mark 5**
- [ ] 14. **2 Samuel 21-22**
- [ ] 15. **2 Samuel 23-24** & **Mark 6**
- [ ] 16. **1 Kings 1-2**
- [ ] 17. **1 Kings 3-4** & **Mark 7**
- [ ] 18. **1 Kings 5-6**
- [ ] 19. **1 Kings 7-8** & **Mark 8**
- [ ] 20. **1 Kings 9-10**
- [ ] 21. **Psalms 61-64**
- [ ] 22. **1 Kings 11-12** & **Mark 9**
- [ ] 23. **1 Kings 13-14**
- [ ] 24. **1 Kings 15-16** & **Mark 10**
- [ ] 25. **1 Kings 17-18**
- [ ] 26. **1 Kings 19-20** & **Mark 11**
- [ ] 27. **1 Kings 21-22** & **Mark 12**
- [ ] 28. **2 Kings 1-2** & **Mark 13**
- [ ] 29. **2 Kings 3-4** & **Mark 14**
- [ ] 30. **Psalms 65-68**
- [ ] 31. **2 Kings 5-6** & **Mark 15**

June

- [ ] 1. **2 Kings 7-8** & **Mark 16**
- [ ] 2. **2 Kings 9-10** & **Luke 1**
- [ ] 3. **2 Kings 11-12** & **Luke 2**

- ☐ 4. **2 Kings 13-14** & **Luke 3**
- ☐ 5. **2 Kings 15-16** & **Luke 4**
- ☐ 6. **2 Kings 17-18** & **Luke 5**
- ☐ 7. **2 Kings 19-20** & **Luke 6**
- ☐ 8. **Psalms 69-72**
- ☐ 9. **2 Kings 21-22** & **Luke 7**
- ☐ 10. **2 Kings 23-25** & **Luke 8**
- ☐ 11. **1 Chronicles 1-2** & **Luke 9**
- ☐ 12. **1 Chronicles 3-4** & **Luke 10**
- ☐ 13. **1 Chronicles 5-6** & **Luke 11**
- ☐ 14. **1 Chronicles 7-8** & **Luke 12**
- ☐ 15. **1 Chronicles 9-10** & **Luke 13**
- ☐ 16. **1 Chronicles 11-12** & **Luke 14**
- ☐ 17. **Psalms 73-76**
- ☐ 18. **1 Chronicles 13-14** & **Luke 15**
- ☐ 19. **1 Chronicles 15-16** & **Luke 16**
- ☐ 20. **1 Chronicles 17-18** & **Luke 17**
- ☐ 21. **1 Chronicles 19-20** & **Luke 18**
- ☐ 22. **1 Chronicles 21-22** & **Luke 19**
- ☐ 23. **1 Chronicles 23-24** & **Luke 20**
- ☐ 24. **1 Chronicles 25-26** & **Luke 21**
- ☐ 25. **1 Chronicles 27-29** & **Luke 22**
- ☐ 26. **Psalms 77-80**
- ☐ 27. **2 Chronicles 1-2** & **Luke 23**
- ☐ 28. **2 Chronicles 3-4** & **Luke 24**
- ☐ 29. **2 Chronicles 5-6** & **Acts 1**
- ☐ 30. **2 Chronicles 7-8** & **Acts 2**

July

- [ ] 1. 2 Chronicles 9-10 & Acts 3
- [ ] 2. 2 Chronicles 11-12 & Acts 4
- [ ] 3. 2 Chronicles 13-14 & Acts 5
- [ ] 4. 2 Chronicles 15-16 & Acts 6
- [ ] 5. Psalms 81-84
- [ ] 6. 2 Chronicles 17-18 & Acts 7
- [ ] 7. 2 Chronicles 19-20 & Acts 8
- [ ] 8. 2 Chronicles 21-22 & Acts 9
- [ ] 9. 2 Chronicles 23-24 & Acts 10
- [ ] 10. 2 Chronicles 25-26 & Acts 11
- [ ] 11. 2 Chronicles 27-28 & Acts 12
- [ ] 12. 2 Chronicles 29-30 & Acts 13
- [ ] 13. 2 Chronicles 31-32 & Acts 14
- [ ] 14. Psalms 85-88
- [ ] 15. 2 Chronicles 33-34 & Acts 15
- [ ] 16. 2 Chronicles 35-36 & Acts 16
- [ ] 17. Ezra 1-2 & Acts 17
- [ ] 18. Ezra 3-4 & Acts 18
- [ ] 19. Ezra 5-6 & Acts 19
- [ ] 20. Ezra 7-8 & Acts 20
- [ ] 21. Ezra 9-10 & Acts 21
- [ ] 22. Psalms 89-92
- [ ] 23. Nehemiah 1-2 & Acts 22
- [ ] 24. Nehemiah 3-4 & Acts 23
- [ ] 25. Nehemiah 5-6 & Acts 24
- [ ] 26. Nehemiah 7-9 & Acts 25

- ☐ 27. **Nehemiah 10-11** & **Acts 26**
- ☐ 28. **Nehemiah 12-13** & **Acts 27**
- ☐ 29. **Esther 1-2** & **Acts 28**
- ☐ 30. **Esther 3-4** & **Romans 1**
- ☐ 31. **Esther 5-7** & **Romans 2**

August

- ☐ 1. **Esther 8-10** & **Romans 3**
- ☐ 2. **Psalms 93-96**
- ☐ 3. **Job 1-3** & **Romans 4**
- ☐ 4. **Job 4-6** & **Romans 5**
- ☐ 5. **Job 7-9** & **Romans 6**
- ☐ 6. **Job 10-12** & **Romans 7**
- ☐ 7. **Job 13-15** & **Romans 8**
- ☐ 8. **Job 16-18** & **Romans 9**
- ☐ 9. **Job 19-21** & **Romans 10**
- ☐ 10. **Psalms 97-100**
- ☐ 11. **Job 22-24** & **Romans 11**
- ☐ 12. **Job 25-27** & **Romans 12**
- ☐ 13. **Job 28-30** & **Romans 13**
- ☐ 14. **Job 31-33** & **Romans 14**
- ☐ 15. **Job 34-36** & **Romans 15**
- ☐ 16. **Job 37-39** & **Romans 16**
- ☐ 17. **Job 40-42** & **1 Corinthians 1**
- ☐ 18. **Proverbs 1-2** & **1 Corinthians 2**
- ☐ 19. **Proverbs 3-4** & **1 Corinthians 3**
- ☐ 20. **Psalms 101-104**
- ☐ 21. **Proverbs 5-7** & **1 Corinthians 4**

- ☐ 22. **Proverbs 8-9** & **1 Corinthians 5**
- ☐ 23. **Proverbs 10-11** & **1 Corinthians 6**
- ☐ 24. **Proverbs 12-13** & **1 Corinthians 7**
- ☐ 25. **Proverbs 14-15** & **1 Corinthians 8**
- ☐ 26. **Proverbs 16-17** & **1 Corinthians 9**
- ☐ 27. **Proverbs 18-19** & **1 Corinthians 10**
- ☐ 28. **Proverbs 20-21** & **1 Corinthians 11**
- ☐ 29. **Proverbs 22-23** & **1 Corinthians 12**
- ☐ 30. **Proverbs 24-25** & **1 Corinthians 13**
- ☐ 31. **Proverbs 26-27** & **1 Corinthians 14**

September

- ☐ 1. **Proverbs 28-29** & **1 Corinthians 15**
- ☐ 2. **Proverbs 30-31** & **1 Corinthians 16**
- ☐ 3. **Ecclesiastes 1-3** & **2 Corinthians 1**
- ☐ 4. **Ecclesiastes 4-6** & **2 Corinthians 2**
- ☐ 5. **Ecclesiastes 7-9** & **2 Corinthians 3**
- ☐ 6. **Ecclesiastes 10-12**
- ☐ 7. **Psalms 105-107**
- ☐ 8. **Psalms 108-110**
- ☐ 9. **Song of Solomon 1-2** & **2 Corinthians 4**
- ☐ 10. **Song of Solomon 3-4** & **2 Corinthians 5**
- ☐ 11. **Song of Solomon 5-6** & **2 Corinthians 6**
- ☐ 12. **Song of Solomon 7-8** & **2 Corinthians 7**
- ☐ 13. **Isaiah 1-3** & **2 Corinthians 8**
- ☐ 14. **Isaiah 4-6** & **2 Corinthians 9**
- ☐ 15. **Isaiah 7-9** & **2 Corinthians 10**
- ☐ 16. **Isaiah 10-12** & **2 Corinthians 11**

- ☐ 17. **Isaiah 13-15** & **2 Corinthians 12**
- ☐ 18. **Isaiah 16-18** & **2 Corinthians 13**
- ☐ 19. **Isaiah 19-21** & **Galatians 1**
- ☐ 20. **Psalms 111-114**
- ☐ 21. **Isaiah 22-24** & **Galatians 2**
- ☐ 22. **Isaiah 25-27** & **Galatians 3**
- ☐ 23. **Isaiah 28-30** & **Galatians 4**
- ☐ 24. **Isaiah 31-33** & **Galatians 5**
- ☐ 25. **Isaiah 34-36** & **Galatians 6**
- ☐ 26. **Isaiah 37-39** & **Ephesians 1**
- ☐ 27. **Isaiah 40-42** & **Ephesians 2**
- ☐ 28. **Isaiah 43-45** & **Ephesians 3**
- ☐ 29. **Isaiah 46-48** & **Ephesians 4**
- ☐ 30. **Isaiah 49-51** & **Ephesians 5**

October

- ☐ 1. **Isaiah 52-54** & **Ephesians 6**
- ☐ 2. **Isaiah 55-57** **Philippians 1**
- ☐ 3. **Psalms 115-118**
- ☐ 4. **Isaiah 58-60** & **Philippians 2**
- ☐ 5. **Isaiah 61-63** & **Philippians 3**
- ☐ 6. **Isaiah 64-66** & **Philippians 4**
- ☐ 7. **Jeremiah 1-3** & **Colossians 1**
- ☐ 8. **Jeremiah 4-6** & **Colossians 2**
- ☐ 9. **Jeremiah 7-9** & **Colossians 3**
- ☐ 10. **Jeremiah 10-12** & **Colossians 4**
- ☐ 11. **Psalm 119**
- ☐ 12. **Psalms 120-122**

- ☐ 13. **Jeremiah 13-15** & **1 Thessalonians 1**
- ☐ 14. **Jeremiah 16-18** & **1 Thessalonians 2**
- ☐ 15. **Jeremiah 19-21** & **1 Thessalonians 3**
- ☐ 16. **Jeremiah 22-24** & **1 Thessalonians 4**
- ☐ 17. **Jeremiah 25-27** & **1 Thessalonians 5**
- ☐ 18. **Jeremiah 28-30** & **2 Thessalonians 1**
- ☐ 19. **Jeremiah 31-33** & **2 Thessalonians 2**
- ☐ 20. **Jeremiah 34-36** & **2 Thessalonians 3**
- ☐ 21. **Psalms 123-126**
- ☐ 22. **Jeremiah 37-39** & **1 Timothy 1**
- ☐ 23. **Jeremiah 40-42** & **1 Timothy 2**
- ☐ 24. **Jeremiah 43-45** & **1 Timothy 3**
- ☐ 25. **Jeremiah 46-48** & **1 Timothy 4**
- ☐ 26. **Jeremiah 49-50** & **1 Timothy 5**
- ☐ 27. **Jeremiah 51-52** & **1 Timothy 6**
- ☐ 28. **Lamentations 1-2** & **2 Timothy 1**
- ☐ 29. **Lamentations 3-5** & **2 Timothy 2**
- ☐ 30. **Ezekiel 1-3** & **2 Timothy 3**
- ☐ 31. **Ezekiel 4-6** & **2 Timothy 4**

November

- ☐ 1. **Ezekiel 7-9** & **Titus 1**
- ☐ 2. **Ezekiel 10-12** & **Titus 2**
- ☐ 3. **Ezekiel 13-15** & **Titus 3**
- ☐ 4. **Ezekiel 16-18** & **Philemon**
- ☐ 5. **Psalm 127-130**
- ☐ 6. **Psalm 131-134**
- ☐ 7. **Ezekiel 19-21** & **Hebrews 1**

- ☐ 8. **Ezekiel 22-24** & **Hebrews 2**
- ☐ 9. **Ezekiel 25-27** & **Hebrews 3**
- ☐ 10. **Ezekiel 28-30** & **Hebrews 4**
- ☐ 11. **Ezekiel 31-33** & **Hebrews 5**
- ☐ 12. **Ezekiel 34-36** & **Hebrews 6**
- ☐ 13. **Ezekiel 37-39** & **Hebrews 7**
- ☐ 14. **Ezekiel 40-42** & **Hebrews 8**
- ☐ 15. **Ezekiel 43-45** & **Hebrews 9**
- ☐ 16. **Ezekiel 46-48** & **Hebrews 10**
- ☐ 17. **Hosea 1-3** & **Hebrews 11**
- ☐ 18. **Hosea 4-6** & **Hebrews 12**
- ☐ 19. **Hosea 7-9** & **Hebrews 13**
- ☐ 20. **Hosea 10-12** & **James 1**
- ☐ 21. **Hosea 13-14** & **James 2**
- ☐ 22. **Joel 1-3** & **James 3**
- ☐ 23. **Amos 1-3** & **James 4**
- ☐ 24. **Amos 4-6** & **James 5**
- ☐ 25. **Psalm 135-138**
- ☐ 26. **Amos 7-9** & **1 Peter 1**
- ☐ 27. **Obadiah** & **1 Peter 2**
- ☐ 28. **Jonah 1-4** & **1 Peter 3**
- ☐ 29. **Micah 1-2** & **1 Peter 4**
- ☐ 30. **Micah 3-5** & **1 Peter 5**

December

- ☐ 1. **Micah 6-7** & **2 Peter 1**
- ☐ 2. **Nahum 1-3** & **2 Peter 2**
- ☐ 3. **Habakkuk 1-3** & **2 Peter 3**

- ☐ 4. **Psalm 139-142**
- ☐ 5. **Zephaniah 1-3** & **1 John 1**
- ☐ 6. **Haggai 1-2** & **1 John 2**
- ☐ 7. **Zechariah 1-3** & **1 John 3**
- ☐ 8. **Zechariah 4-6** & **1 John 4**
- ☐ 9. **Zechariah 7-9** & **1 John 5**
- ☐ 10. **Zechariah 10-12** & **2 John**
- ☐ 11. **Zechariah 13-14** & **3 John**
- ☐ 12. **Malachi 1-4** & **Jude**
- ☐ 13. **Psalm 143-146**
- ☐ 14. **Daniel 1-2**
- ☐ 15. **Daniel 3-4**
- ☐ 16. **Daniel 5-6**
- ☐ 17. **Daniel 7-8**
- ☐ 18. **Daniel 9-10**
- ☐ 19. **Daniel 11-12**
- ☐ 20. **Psalm 147-150**
- ☐ 21. **Revelation 1-2**
- ☐ 22. **Revelation 3-4**
- ☐ 23. **Revelation 5-6**
- ☐ 24. **Revelation 7-8**
- ☐ 25. **Revelation 9-10**
- ☐ 26. **Revelation 11-12**
- ☐ 27. **Revelation 13-14**
- ☐ 28. **Revelation 15-16**
- ☐ 29. **Revelation 17-18**
- ☐ 30. **Revelation 19-20**
- ☐ 31. **Revelation 21-22**

Devotional #1

Is Life Supposed to Be This Hard?

In the course of our Christian journey, we generally find ourselves in one of three states. We've either just come through a trial, we're in the midst of a trial, or we're about to face a new trial.

The writer of James 1:2-4 instructs us: "Count it all joy my brethren, when you encounter various trials, knowing that the testing of your faith produces endurance. And let endurance have its perfect result, that you may be perfect and complete, lacking in nothing." But it's not easy to "count it all joy" when we find ourselves in the midst of pain and suffering.

Yet, our heavenly Father is faithful to His Word. Paul assures us in 2 Corinthians 3:18, that God daily transforms us from glory to glory, into the perfect image of Jesus Christ. God did not remove the cup of suffering from His Beloved Son, Who was obedient to the point of death. Can we ask for an easier path than the one willingly taken by our blessed Savior?

Take heart in the midst of suffering. Your trials are not strange things that have come upon you. God is on His throne and not a single detail escapes His watchful eye where His children are concerned. Jesus, our High Priest, is sympathetic to your grief and He is touched by your sorrows. Nothing in your life is too insignificant to bring to Him and place at the cross.

Perhaps you've been guilty of telling God, "I don't want to face this trial. Please release me from it." Try praying this instead: "Father, please help me respond to this trial in a way that pleases and glories You." Tell Him that you want your heart always to be one that says, "Yes Lord!" God is your ever-present help in time of need.

"Father, I welcome the trials in my life as opportunities to become more like Jesus Christ. Bring them on Lord. I trust You."

Devotional #2
Making Sense Out of Suffering

Nothing is wasted in God's economy. He faithfully uses every experience you face in life to conform you to His image. Think of the most difficult situation you are facing today. Perhaps you're overwhelmed by the magnitude of the problem. First, try writing it down. This often helps to prevent thinking in "circles," and sometimes narrows the scope of the pain.

Have you wondered if this one's too big even for God? Maybe you find it hard to accomplish even your basic daily responsibilities because all your emotional energy is focused on this burden. You feel spiritually drained, and you can't even envision a time in the future when your heart will no longer be weighed down by the pain of this circumstance.

Faith and hope are inseparable qualities for the Believer. If you are determined to live your life by faith rather than by sight, you must first decide to obey His Word regardless of the personal cost. Welcome your present suffering as an opportunity to demonstrate your reliance upon His goodness.

Make the words of Psalm 5:1,2 your own: "Give ear to my words, Lord. Consider my groaning. Heed the sound of my cry for help, my King and my God." Draw comfort from Psalm 5:3: "In the morning, Lord, You will hear my voice." Cry out to Him when you awaken each day. Trust that God is able to restore hope to your discouraged heart!

Lay hold of the glorious promise found in Romans 8:28: "We know that God causes all things to work together for good to those who love God, to those who are called according to His purpose." Take renewed confidence that God is in control. He *can* be trusted to work out *every* detail of this trial, for your good and His glory.

"Lord, please use my present trials to build the qualities of faith and hope into my life."

Devotional #3

How Can I Love Someone Who Hurts Me?

The most amazing thing about God's love is that He chose to love us while we were yet His enemies. He didn't wait until we became lovable to declare His unconditional love for us.

Are there people in your life who are hard to love? Does it sometimes seem the more you try to reach out to him or her, the more you open yourself up to pain and heartache? Difficult people are part of our lives by God's design, not by chance. Our Heavenly Father wants us to learn to love others as He loves us.

The writer of 1 Corinthians 13:4 tells us that patience is an integral part of loving someone. Patience has been aptly defined as accepting difficult situations from God and responding to them correctly. Learning to love problematic individuals is a key aspect of the Christian experience. Don't be guilty of giving God a deadline to remove trying situations and relationships from your life.

People who love others are willing to make themselves vulnerable. Are you transparent about your failures as well as your strengths? Will you love enough to open your life to the possibility of insults, and perhaps rejection? Will you continue to love others with the love of Christ, even in the face of betrayal?

Godly love gives to the needs of others without expecting anything in return. When your neighbor offends you, you must love him as much as you love yourself, according to Leviticus 19:18. When your enemy hurts you, you need to obey the command found in Matthew 5:44, and love him in spite of your pain.

God leaves us no option but to love. The opposite of love is selfishness, and believers have a clear scriptural command to do nothing from selfishness or empty conceit.

Rather, we are humbly to regard one another as more important than ourselves. Only then will we love unlovable people as Jesus Christ loves us.

"Dear Lord, make me a lover of others and not a lover of self."

Devotional #4

Don't Ever Give Up!

Is the trial you're facing today threatening to undo you? Has the weight of the burden you're carrying worn you down and are you tempted to call it quits? Have you begun to think that it's no longer worth the effort you're investing to see the problem through?

Be encouraged with these words from Hebrews 12:1,2: "Let us lay aside every encumbrance, and the sin which so easily entangles us, and let us run with endurance the race that is set before us, fixing our eyes on Jesus, the author and perfecter of our faith."

Dear Christian, do not grow weary in obeying God. Keep doing good deeds for those people who persecute you. Don't allow your heart to be embittered against them. Continue to pray for those who seek to harm you. Refuse to give up! Remember that the Lord began a good work in you at salvation and He will be faithful to continue that work, and ultimately to complete it.

According to James 1:12, you qualify to one day receive a crown of life when you choose to persevere. God has promised this glorious crown to every Believer who loves Him enough to endure to the end, no matter how difficult the circumstances.

In the midst of this trial, seek to learn well the lessons of endurance and determination. Purpose to accomplish that which God expects, regardless of the difficulties you're facing. He cares deeply about the pressure and stress you're undergoing, and He will give you the inward strength necessary to withstand it. God will enable you to keep going in order to accomplish His best in your life. Best of all, His name will be glorified.

"Father, today I commit myself anew to the truth that quitting is not an option for a Christian."

Devotional #5

Only God Gives Us His Peace

As our frenetic society is propelled along at an ever-increasing speed, it's not unusual for Christians to experience fear, anxiety, or even panic. When your life is overcome by worry and fear you may have difficulty sleeping, eating, or even performing the smallest tasks of your daily routine.

In a word, you feel paralyzed. God addresses this malady very specifically in Philippians 4:6,7: "Be anxious for nothing, but in everything by prayer and supplication with thanksgiving, let your requests be made known to God. And the peace of God, which surpasses all comprehension, shall guard your hearts and minds in Christ Jesus."

Most of us know certain individuals who seem to have an inner calm and radiance. We're drawn to them and we feel encouraged and spiritually energized when we're in their presence.

On the other hand, we tend to avoid people who have a reputation for self-pity. Their "hang-dog" countenance and negative attitude gradually sap our vitality and zest. Just spending time with them leaves us feeling spiritually drained.

How do those radiant people get to be that way? How do we? Only by appropriating the peace of God. By structuring our life around the things that are eternal and can't be destroyed or taken away.

A Believer who finds peace in the security of worldly possessions, a good job, or even a wonderfully satisfying relationship, is headed for certain disillusionment and disappointment.

You are God's creation and He demands first place in your heart. He will settle for nothing less! And He will sacrifice whatever is necessary in your life to press you into Himself.

You will find peace in nothing and no one other than Jesus Christ. He has reconciled you to God by His death and resurrection. He *is* your peace. Today allow God's peace to guard your heart and mind.

"Lord God, You alone are my peace. Whenever I am anxious or afraid today, I will trust in You."

Devotional #6
An Attitude of Gratitude

Our culture seems to be plagued with a pervasive dose of ingratitude. We don't appreciate good service. We expect it! We don't *prefer* to be treated courteously. We demand it! When we're inconvenienced in the slightest way, we protest loudly. We've grown accustomed to instant gratification.

Luke 17:11-19 describes a stunning incident that occurred during Jesus' earthly ministry. After Jesus healed ten lepers, they all went on their way. One, however, remembered to come back to thank Him. When he returned to express his heartfelt gratitude, Jesus questioned him: "Were there not ten cleansed? But the nine—where are they? Was no one found who turned back to give glory to God except you?"

The writer of Psalm 91:1-3 affirms: "It is good to give thanks to the Lord, and to sing praises to Your name, Oh Most High; to declare Your loving kindness in the morning, and Your faithfulness by night." The leper who returned to Jesus didn't come timidly or quietly. When he saw that he had been healed, he turned back with a loud voice and fell at Jesus' feet, giving Him emotion-filled thanks.

Starting today, make an earnest effort to demonstrate a grateful spirit. First, spend time thanking God for specific blessings you've received from His hand. Sing praises of thanksgiving to your loving Heavenly Father. Don't be ashamed to lift your voice audibly to Him in grateful adoration.

Decide within your heart that you won't be like the nine ungrateful lepers who went their way with no word of thanks for God's goodness to them. Be alert for opportunities to express to others, the specific ways they've benefited your life and ministered to you. Make a brief phone call, send an email, or write a note telling someone how much you appreciate his or her investment in your life.

"Lord, I want to be like the one leper who returned to Jesus with thanksgiving."

Devotional #7

Taking Responsibility for My Life

Countless people in today's world have bought into a "victim" mentality. They blame their failures and irresponsible behavior on other people. They're convinced they can't possibly be whole, or ever lead successful lives because of all the bad things that have happened to them throughout their lives.

Schoolteachers were unfair, friends made fun of them, parents didn't love them enough, employers won't give them the breaks they deserved, and their spouse doesn't understand them. In short, they've been cheated and mistreated. Their shortcomings are just not their fault.

This kind of thinking leads a person straight into the pit of depression and self-pity. Jesus tells us in Matthew 5:45: "God causes His sun to rise on the evil and the good, and sends rain on the righteous and the unrighteous."

When Christ redeems us from our sin, He does not, thereby, guarantee us a painless life of ease. He hasn't promised His children immunity from trials and suffering. The truth is, Christians live in a fallen world. In this life, we will experience sorrow, but God has promised to be with us and to strengthen us in the midst of our sorrow and tribulation. He is our refuge and our help in time of need.

One particular passage of Jesus' High Priestly prayer in John 17 makes it clear that Christians must live in this evil world. Jesus asks His Father to keep Believers from the Evil One, but He does not ask God to *remove* them from the possibility of suffering while they live on this earth.

Are you blaming others for your failures and shortcomings? This day, determine that you will no longer practice the fruitless and unbiblical habit of blame-shifting. Instead, take responsibility for cheerfully doing those things that God and others are expecting from you.

"Lord, I take responsibility for my every thought, word, and action. I won't blame my failures or faults on anyone else."

Devotional #8

Work is Honorable!

An alarming number of people today seem not to have a very strong work ethic. Any time you're out shopping, or at a fast food restaurant, for example, you're likely to hear employees complaining loudly and unreservedly about their jobs—to their co-workers, or even to the customers!

This appears to be the consensus: do the minimum amount of work required to "get by" and avoid hard work whenever possible. If you do get assigned the hard jobs, be sure to gripe about it. (If you're really irritated, maybe even throw in a few obscenities!)

But God's Word stands in direct opposition to this kind of thinking. The writer of Proverbs 19:15 warns: "Laziness casts into a deep sleep, and an idle man will suffer hunger." Have you ever noted the fact that Adam and Eve's fall from God's grace had not yet happened when God charged Adam with the job of taking care of the Garden of Eden?

Listen again to the account in Genesis 2:15: "Then the Lord God took the man and put him into the Garden of Eden to cultivate it and keep it." Work was not a punishment for sin. It was a noble calling that God lovingly entrusted to mankind.

Do your children hear you complain about your work responsibilities? Have you repented? Do your children complain about their own chores? Hasten to remind them of Paul's sobering admonition to the church at Thessalonica: "If anyone will not work, neither let him eat."

Do you often find yourself dreading the work that faces you each day? Be warned by these words from Proverbs 6:9-11: "How long will you lie down, Oh sluggard? When will you arise from your sleep? 'A little sleep, a little slumber, a little folding of the hands to rest, and your poverty will come upon you.' "

There is great dignity in labor, but the penalty for slothfulness is poverty. Begin today to visualize each task you face as a special assignment from God. Attempt to use all your energies to accomplish each job in an excellent manner. As Scripture puts it: "Whatever your hand finds to do, do it with all your might!" No half-heartedness allowed! If you're faithful in carrying out small assignments, God will begin to entrust you with bigger ones.

Here's another suggestion. As you undertake each new task, try to leave evidence of having done *more* than what was required of you. Does that sound crazy? Not at all! Remember, you're doing your work as unto the Lord Jesus Christ.

"Lord, I desire to work diligently and uncomplainingly today on every task set before me."

Devotional #9
Lord, it's Hard to Be Humble!

The angel Lucifer, "Star of the Morning, Son of the Dawn," was cast out of heaven because He wanted to be like the Most High God. Satan was guilty of the sin of pride. Within every human heart, there is the desire to be admired and respected.

We want our work to be acknowledged and our accomplishments to be recognized. We may even lose sleep worrying about what people think about us. We go to great lengths to defend our personal reputation should it, for any reason, be questioned.

Pride is a quality that is valued and encouraged by our society. God, however, requires that His children walk humbly before Him. Jesus Christ is our supreme example of humility. The writer of Philippians 2:5-8 advises: "Have this attitude in yourselves which was also in Christ Jesus, who, although He existed in the form of God, did not regard equality with God a thing to be grasped, but emptied Himself, taking the form of a bond-servant. . .and became obedient to the point of death, even death on a cross."

By an act of faith, give your reputation to God. Cast yourself upon His mercy and allow Him to be your defense. When you are tempted to take credit for a particular accomplishment or success, remember that any good in your life is the result of God's grace alone. Be obedient to the scriptural command to "let another man's lips praise you, and not your own."

We learn in James 4:6 that God is opposed to the proud, but He gives grace to the humble. Humility of spirit renders us eligible for God's grace, and if God be for us, who can be against us?

"Dear Lord, subdue my proud heart and remind me that apart from You, I am nothing."

Devotional #10
Forgive Seventy Times Seven?

Matthew 18:21,22 records an amazing exchange between Jesus and Peter, His outspoken disciple: "Then Peter came and said to Him, 'Lord, how often shall my brother sin against me and I forgive him? Up to seven times?' Jesus said to him, 'I do not say to you up to seven times, but up to seventy times seven.'"

Imagine Peter's astonishment at Jesus' answer. Peter doubtlessly believed he had cleverly figured out the whole forgiveness issue. In the Jewish religion the number seven represented perfection. It's likely that Peter was convinced his response was even brilliant. After all, his suggestion far exceeded the minimum requirement for forgiving others.

Yet, Jesus countered Peter's proposal with a command that eliminated any possibility for scorekeeping. His answer to Peter underscored the principle that God commands us to forgive our offenders an infinite number of times. We simply aren't allowed to count.

Not forgiving is *not* an option for Christians. A Believer who has been offended has no choice but to forgive. The writer of Ephesians 4:32 instructs us to forgive others just as God in Christ has forgiven us. Dare we withhold forgiveness from an offender when we ourselves have been forgiven so great a debt of sin?

In the Old Testament story, Joseph demonstrated his keen grasp of biblical forgiveness when he revealed his identity to his brothers. They trembled before him when they realized who he was, terrified that he would now seek revenge for the wrongs they had cruelly inflicted upon him years earlier.

Joseph, however, explained to them that although their intentions toward him were evil, God's sovereign will was being accomplished in his life. Joseph harbored no resentment or lack of forgiveness toward his brothers. Rather, he acknowledged God's Hand at work in the midst of their evil deeds.

We must never attribute evil to Holy God. He is not the author of evil. But be assured that if you belong to Him, nothing can touch your life unless God first authorizes it.

Today, as you encounter various offenses, try to respond to them lovingly. Remember that God allows each circumstance to occur in your life for a specific purpose. Then take the necessary biblical steps to deal properly with the offenses. Don't miss the extraordinary lesson He has in store for you this day!

"Lord God, cleanse my heart of all bitterness and teach me to forgive as You forgive."

Devotional #11

Speaking With Gentleness and Kindness

Spoken words have a powerful effect upon our lives. Words can edify and uplift us, or they can emotionally wound and deflate us. Can you recall a particular incident in your life when someone's unkind words pierced your heart and seemed to rip the very foundation from beneath you?

The writer of Proverbs 25:11 tells us that a word spoken in right circumstances is like "apples of gold in settings of silver." The spirit in which we speak is also vitally important. Part of God's requirement for His children in Micah 6:8 is the command to love kindness. Are you sometimes tempted to speak harshly to your friends, family members, or coworkers? Do you make an effort to temper the tone of your voice with the gentleness of Jesus Christ?

Have you considered whether your facial expressions reflect the loving-kindness of the Lord? We find that both kindness and gentleness appear on the Galatians 5 "Fruit of the Spirit" list. Christians must never justify harsh attitudes or unkind words.

Paul emphasizes the importance of gentleness in Ephesians 4:1,2. He urges Believers to "walk in a manner worthy of their calling, with all humility and gentleness." Proverbs 31 also points to the importance of kindness. Verse 26 describes a godly woman as one who "opens her mouth in wisdom and the teaching of kindness is on her tongue."

God instructs us in Colossians 3:12, as those who have been chosen of God to "put on a heart of compassion, kindness, humility, gentleness and patience." The gentleness and kindness you demonstrate today may be a profound encouragement to someone who needs, as Romans 11:22 puts it, "to behold the kindness of God."

"Lord, I long to demonstrate the qualities of gentleness and kindness in my life. Make me a vessel of humility and patience."

Devotional #12
The Danger of Favoritism

The writer of Galatians 2:6 comforts us with this promise, "God shows no partiality." Indeed, God does not play favorites. His goodness and mercy are available in full measure to every Christian who wholeheartedly seeks after Him. The Lord assures us in Jeremiah 29:13: "You will seek Me and find Me when you search for Me with all your heart."

God's ways, however, are higher than our ways and we are often guilty of the sin of favoritism in our relationships with one another. Isaac made no secret of the fact that he had singled out Esau as his favorite son. Rebecca, on the other hand, openly favored Esau's brother Jacob.

Tragically, their sins of favoritism were carried on to the next generation. Jacob angered all his other sons by the partiality he showed to young Joseph. Years earlier, Jacob had covetously lied and tricked his own brother, Esau. Jacob's sons, following their father's poor example, also jealously lied and even cruelly plotted to kill their brother Joseph.

We read this exhortation in Proverbs 28:21: "To show partiality is not good." Are there relationships in your life that need mending? Have situations arisen wherein you've failed to give just consideration to all parties concerned? Have you sought to understand the viewpoint of each person involved, with impartiality? We find this stern warning in Galatians 6:7: "Do not be deceived, God is not mocked; for whatever a man sows, this he will also reap."

Jealousy, strife and contention are the inevitable outcomes of showing partiality. You cannot show special favor to those within your scope of care and influence, without paying a costly price. Today, ask the Lord to reveal to you any favoritism residing within your heart. Purpose to take the necessary steps to seek forgiveness of the people involved, and in God's strength, begin the journey toward reconciliation.

"Father, teach me to love others with the impartial love of God."

Devotional #13
Are You Content?

The words of Philippians 2:14 are a formidable challenge to the heart of every Christian: "Do all things without grumbling or disputing, that you may prove yourselves to be blameless and innocent, children of God above reproach in the midst of a crooked and perverse generation." We seem to love to complain. At times, we even compete to top one another's tales of woe. Sometimes it feels great to elaborate on how hard we have it at home, or how impossible our employer has become, or how horribly a friend or family member is treating us.

Most of us haven't yet learned the secret of contentment. Paul's life offers us insight into this pursuit. He states in Philippians 4:11-13: "I have learned to be content in whatever circumstances I am…in any and every circumstance I have learned the secret…I can do all things through Him who strengthens me."

Here was a man who survived imprisonment, false accusations, stoning, hunger, bitter cold, brutal beatings, shipwreck, and the bite of a venomous snake. Nevertheless, he was content in *each* one of those situations.

God is a tender and watchful Shepherd. All the sheep of His pasture can be confident that He faithfully attends to every need of His flock. God does not conceal the plans that He has for His children. He tells us in Jeremiah 29:11: "I know the plans that I have for you; plans for welfare and not for calamity to give you a future and a hope.

In the Old Testament, Job admits at one point, that his complaining is rebellion against God. Ultimately Job cries, "Though He slay me, I will hope in Him!" May your faith in God's provision be so steadfast that regardless of whatever circumstances you encounter, you will find your contentment in the Lord Jesus Christ.

"Lord Jesus, keep me from the sin of complaining and teach me contentment in You."

Devotional #14

Speaking the Truth in Love

We Christians seem to find it easy to exaggerate the facts, stretch the truth, or tell what's called a "little white lie." Perhaps the reason we take the liberty to embellish facts or a story in the retelling, is to make it a bit more intriguing—a little "juicier." However, we need to face the truth that God in no way endorses *any* of these practices.

The writer of Ephesians 4:25 firmly admonishes: "Therefore, laying aside falsehood, speak truth, each one of you, with his neighbor, for we are members of one another." When we strive to report the facts of a situation truthfully, without seeking to enhance them, we earn a reputation for being honest. Others come to trust us and to rely upon the accuracy of our words.

We find these instructions in 1 Peter 1:22: "Since you have, in obedience to the truth, purified your souls for a sincere love of the brethren, fervently love one another from the heart." Peter continues by telling us to put aside all hypocrisy.

A sincere person is one whose motives are transparent. He has no hidden agenda of self-promotion for he has learned the secret of loving others selflessly. He understands the joy of endeavoring to make others successful.

Here's how God describes a liar in Proverbs 6:12: "A worthless person, a wicked man, is the one who walks with a false mouth." But what about a flatterer? That's harmless enough, isn't it? Not if you believe this description in Psalm 5: "They flatter with their tongue. Their throat is an open grave."

A false witness and a flatterer are, in God's estimation, of no value to Him. Instead, He wants us to obey His command in Ephesians 4:15: "Speaking the truth in love, we are to grow up in all aspects into Him who is the Head, even Christ."

"Dear Lord, please restrain my lips from flattery and lies, and teach me to speak the truth lovingly."

Devotional #15

Prefer One Another In Love

Rude behavior is rampant in today's society. Radios blare loudly from passing vehicles. People don't hesitate to shout foul language and gesture obscenely at the slightest provocation. Customer service representatives seem to have lost all perception of providing "service with a smile." Hardly anyone *defers* to others anymore.

What exactly does it mean to *defer*? Deference is the opposite of rudeness. When we defer to others, we voluntarily limit our freedom so we don't offend the tastes of those God has called us to serve. We don't wait for others to conform their lives to our wishes and preferences. Instead, we willingly practice the lovely art, as someone has described it, of "moving over."

Paul teaches us in Philippians 2:3 that we are to regard one another as more important than ourselves. A Christian who wants to obey this command must understand the importance of discretion—a commitment to avoid words, actions, and attitudes that could lead to undesirable circumstances.

We find an amazing promise in Proverbs 3:21-24. The Christian who pursues wisdom and discretion has God's assurance that "they will be life to his soul…his foot will not stumble, when he lies down he will not be afraid and his sleep will be sweet." Acting foolishly and indiscreetly robs us of peace and rest, according to these verses of Scripture.

We find an unforgettable word picture of indiscretion in Proverbs 11:22: "A beautiful woman who lacks discretion is like a ring in a pig's snout." When King David charged his son Solomon with the task of building the Temple, he included in his moving prayer, a request that God would grant Solomon discretion and understanding. Today, come before the Lord God in humility and ask Him to teach you how to exercise deference and discretion in your relationships.

"Holy Spirit I beseech You to make discretion and deference living qualities in my life."

Devotional #16

Be Filled With Praise

We learn in God's Word that the Lord inhabits the praises of His people. When your heart is discouraged by your circumstances and you're tempted to grumble and complain against the Lord, praise is the best remedy.

When you praise your Heavenly Father, you are reminded that He is your Creator and you are His workmanship. Praise has the power to lift you out of your self-focused despondency, and turn your attention upward to the glory and majesty of God. You see, it's absolutely impossible to praise God, and murmur against Him at the same time.

God is the Almighty Holy One. That He should choose to indwell our praises is an astounding truth! We adore Him because His mercy and grace are unending. We love Him because He drew us back to Himself through Christ Jesus, when we were yet enemies and wayward rebels. He is full of tender loving-kindness, and for this, we praise Him.

In the Old Testament, the Psalmist cries out: "Let my mouth be filled with Your praise." Do you want to be full of praise to God? Then you'll need to answer this important question: Are you harboring unconfessed sin in your life? If so, your praise for God will be hindered.

If you're not praising God this day, these questions should help you resume an attitude of praise: Have you confessed every known sin to God and sought His forgiveness? Have you made all your relationships with others right? Is your highest aim to glorify God above all things?

Are you depending on the Holy Spirit's guidance, and will you trust God by faith, even though you can't see evidence of progress? Finally, will you praise God no matter what happens? He alone is worthy of our continual offering of praise.

"Lord, only You can subdue my selfish desires and fill my heart and mouth with praise."

Devotional #17
Growing in the Flames

Everyone needs the encouragement and accountability of a kindred spirit—a Christian friend to whom we can entrust our innermost heart. As we prayerfully seek that intimate fellowship, we gravitate toward people who demonstrate compassion and who possess spiritual depth, don't we? We're drawn to those individuals who have been through God's refining fire, as described in Malachi 3:2.

This kind of person has something to offer of eternal value. He has yielded his heart to the Lord's painful, yet purifying process of burning the dross from his life, and refining the gold that remains by His grace. He has learned the secret of counting it all joy when he encounters trials of various kinds. His countenance reflects the beauty of Jesus Christ—an unmistakable appearance that radiates the peace of God.

These are Believers who know the Lord intimately as their Buckler, their Shield, and their Strong Tower of Refuge. They are steadfast in the face of suffering. They persevere in the midst of hardships, and they will not be moved.

They know God as the One Who causes them to confidently stand, upheld by His righteousness. They are not bewildered by the fiery trials that occur in their lives, because they believe and embrace God's promise that they are being made partners with Jesus Christ in His suffering.

Do you want to know the sanctifying power of the Refiner's fire? Then make the prayer of Philippians 3:10 your own: "That I may know Christ and the power of His resurrection and the fellowship of sharing in His sufferings, becoming like Him in His death." God has lovingly designed the fire in order to make you more like His Beloved Son. You won't grow spiritually apart from the Refiner's fire. And you can rest assured that the flames will not harm you. They'll make you better fit for His use!

"Oh Lord, I want to know You in Your power, and I want to identify with You in Your suffering."

Devotional #18
Growing Deeper in Christ

Many Christians are confused about their purpose in life. They agonize over their future, and they're frustrated by an inability to figure out which direction to take. They seek out counselors and spend untold hours trying to discern their "calling."

If you're discouraged because you can't seem to determine exactly what it is you're to do with your life, the answer is "anything," as long as you obey the Great Commandment! Consider the words of Jesus: "Love the Lord your God with all your soul, with all your mind, and with all your strength. Also, love your neighbor as yourself." This commandment provides a dictate for every relationship we are a part of, and for everything we undertake in life.

God wants you to spend time loving Him and getting to know Him intimately. He desires to fill you so full of His love and grace that wherever you are, whatever you're doing, you will function as *light* to illumine the surrounding darkness, and as *salt* to help preserve a dying world.

You shouldn't focus your energies on seeking a ministry. Instead, seek God's face and allow His Word to radically change your life. Read books of excellence that will mentor and shape your life for righteousness. Meet with godly role models who will disciple you in the faith. As you work diligently to deepen your message, God will broaden the scope of your ministry.

Don't allow your life to be ruled by the "tyranny of the urgent." Submit your schedule to God's scrutiny. Ask Him to reveal to you whether or not each activity you're involved in lines up with scriptural priorities. Then ask yourself, "In light of eternity, how important is this next thing at hand?" Get busy this day carrying out God's agenda. As someone has suggested: Do what *you* can do. Do what you *can* do. All for God's glory.

"Father, I long to love You more every hour and to grow deeper in You each day that I live."

Devotional #19

Become a Servant

Have you ever prayed, "Father God, let others see Jesus in me?" God's Word describes Jesus as a "suffering servant." Are you a servant, known for your love and good deeds? Are you eager to cheerfully lay your life down for others?

When God calls on you to be flexible with your schedule and your plans, do you often feel irritated? Is it hard for you to "prefer someone else in love?" When you don't succeed in getting your way, do you quickly "move over," or do you stiffen your neck and sulk, stubbornly standing your ground?

Jesus instructs us in Matthew 20:26: "If you want to be great in God's kingdom, learn to be a servant of all." Pray that God will give you opportunities to learn how to treat others as more important than yourself. Be willing to wash feet in Jesus' name. Remember that Jesus did not regard His equality with God as something to be grasped or flaunted. But He laid down His Kingly status for our sakes, even to the point of a cruel death on a cross.

The writer of 1 John 3:16 tells us: "We know love by this, that He laid down His life for us and we ought to lay down our lives for the brethren." Although it goes against your fleshly inclinations, God wants you to be willing, for Jesus' sake, to set aside your agenda, your hopes, and your dreams, in order to make the people you are called to serve, successful.

This day, ask the Lord for the grace to obey the directive of Galatians 6:10: "So then, while we have the opportunity, let us do good to all men, and especially to those who are of the household of faith." Today, tell God you are willing to be broken like bread and poured out like wine for His sake.

"Dear Lord, I ask you develop in me a servant's heart."

Devotional #20
Do Not Have Idle Hands

Do you frequently get depressed when you have a long list of things to accomplish in what seems to be an impossibly short period of time? It's not uncommon for some people to become so overwhelmed just thinking about all they're facing emotionally, or all they have to get done, that they shut down and do nothing. They are, in a sense, emotionally paralyzed.

Let's be very plainspoken here. There's no escaping the fact that irresponsibility is a major source of depression! Initially, someone gets behind in his schedule. Next, he begins to feel pressured. Then defeated, to the point of giving up. As a result, he starts to spiral downward emotionally, convinced he can never "dig out from under the pile." Matters grow progressively worse as he continues to fall farther and farther behind in his responsibilities. Soon, he's completely defeated!

If you find yourself in this state, recognize these thoughts as outright lies from Satan: "There's no use in trying. I'll never catch up." Instead obey the exhortation of Ecclesiastes 9:10: "Whatever your hand finds to do, do it with all your might." Don't allow yourself to become immobilized by your "to do" list!

Begin with one task and approach it with diligence and enthusiasm. Then, continue to proceed in this manner until you have fulfilled the responsibilities God requires of you. You will begin to climb out of the pit of despair that formerly threatened to engulf you.

Finally, take the time to get organized. You can't afford not to, if you truly want to obey God's command to "redeem the time." Today, determine those things that hinder you from ministering effectively. Identify the obstacles that prevent you from accomplishing God's agenda. Finally, ask Him for the strength and grace to take care of them. Starting right now!

"Oh Lord, teach me how to redeem the time, and how to be effective for your kingdom!"

Devotional #21
God Gives Beauty for Ashes

Many Christian parents today are guilt-ridden because they failed to raise their children in the nurture and admonition of the Lord. Perhaps they came to Christ themselves when their children were older. Or maybe they didn't understand how to train their children biblically. They feel deeply discouraged by the belief that they've permanently missed their chance to influence their children's lives spiritually.

Well, here's some wonderful news—our Heavenly Father is the God of second chances. Those who genuinely repent before the Lord find a glorious promise in Isaiah 61:3: "God will give you beauty instead of ashes, the oil of joy instead of mourning, and a garment of praise, instead of a spirit of heaviness." If you haven't already done so, approach your adult children in a spirit of humility, and ask their forgiveness for failing them spiritually when they were growing up. Trust God to build new bridges between you and them.

God wants His children to have a vision for three generations. His Word instructs us: "Teach these things to your children and your children's children." If you're a grandparent, read Bible stories to your grandkids. Memorize Scripture with them. Make up fun hand motions to help you remember the verses. Sing praise choruses and the great hymns of the faith together. Make simple costumes and act out scenes with them, from the Old and New Testaments.

If you don't have any children or grandchildren, pour your life into the children who attend your church or who live near you. Let them know that other Christian adults care deeply for them. You have the opportunity to shape their future and to speak into their lives in a unique way. Today, determine that you won't waste one more hour in regret!

"Dear God, I don't want to lose precious time in needless regret. Please restore the years the locusts have eaten away."

Devotional #22
Iron Sharpens Iron

Proverbs 17:17 reminds us that a friend loves at all times. God didn't design us to live in a vacuum. Nowhere in Scripture do we find a "Lone Ranger" style Christianity. We all need close friends who are committed to encouraging us in our Christian walk, and who desire to see us grow in the Lord.

We need friends who know us thoroughly, and yet love us anyway. Heart-mates that help us persevere in times of hardship, and "hold our toes to the fire" when we grow faint-hearted and want to give up.

We read an inspiring account of biblical friendship in the book of 1 Samuel. Jonathan loved David as he loved himself, and their souls were knit together in friendship. Jonathan, who was the heir to his father's throne, made a covenant with David and selflessly risked his own life for his friend.

The writer of Proverbs 27:17 tells us: "As iron sharpens iron, so one man sharpens the countenance of his friend." This verse addresses the wonderful reciprocity of godly friendship. A friend is a mirror that God holds in front of us to help us grow in grace, and to lovingly speak the truth to us.

Be careful that you don't let pride stand in the way of heeding your friend's wise counsel. As God tells us in His Word, the faithful wounds of a friend are better than the kisses of a flatterer.

Today, thank God for the friends He has given you. Do not allow the sin of self-sufficiency to rob you of the joy of intimate biblical friendship. Pray for your friends. Love them unconditionally, and ask the Lord to show you specific ways you can encourage them in their spiritual walk.

"Lord, I treasure the friends that you have given me. Help me to love them selflessly and not to take them for granted."

Devotional #23
Don't Neglect Prayer

Prayer is a means of grace that Christians often neglect. Do you ever feel you're too busy to go to the Lord in prayer? Or perhaps you don't know how to pray. For whatever reason, have you failed to obey the command found in Philippians 4:6? "Be anxious for nothing, but in everything by prayer and supplication with thanksgiving let your requests be made known to God."

Take time today just to contemplate God's glorious nature. Thank Him for Who He is. Praise Him for His majesty, His holiness, and His goodness. Nothing pleases the Lord more than the adoring worship of a grateful, regenerate heart.

Be certain that you're approaching God as a clean vessel, by rigorous and honest self-examination. Ask the Holy Spirit to penetrate to the depths of your being and reveal to you, any sin and corruption that have taken up residence in your heart. In a spirit of repentance, specifically confess, one by one, all the aspects of your life that are disobedient and displeasing to your Heavenly Father.

Next, give thanks to Him in prayer. Remember the mighty things that the Lord has done. Ingratitude is one of the most grievous sins a Christian can commit. Recount your blessings aloud to the Lord so you will "forget not His benefits."

Come before Him with your requests for your own life. He takes joy in binding up the brokenhearted. Boldly present your intercessory prayers for other people. Ask God to move you with compassion as you lift up their needs to Him. We are most like Jesus when we intercede for others.

Finally, try writing out your praises and requests so you'll have a record of God's answers to your prayers throughout your life. You will cherish your "journal of blessings" in the years to come.

"Father, renew in my heart this day, a fervent desire to be a prayer warrior for Your kingdom. Teach me to pray ceaselessly."

Devotional #24

The Lord is Our Shepherd

What reassurance to know that we are God's own people, and the sheep of His pasture! Although sheep aren't very smart animals, they quickly become accustomed to the unique voice of their shepherd. They are indifferent to other voices, but they respond to the loving voice that feeds, cares for, sustains, disciplines, and shelters them.

Jesus is the Good Shepherd Who gave His life for the sheep. In John 10, we read that the sheep hear His voice and He calls His own sheep by name. He goes before them and the sheep follow Him because they know His voice. They trust that He knows best how to care for them.

Do you recognize the voice of your Shepherd? He speaks to His children in many ways. God speaks to us clearly in His Word to communicate to us His purposes and intentions for our lives. He speaks to us through sermons and through godly friends. He speaks majestically through the splendor of His created universe. The writer of Psalm 19 eloquently declares: "The heavens are telling the glory of God. They are a marvelous display of His craftsmanship."

Do you hear God when He speaks to you? Is your heart attuned to "the still, small voice" of the Holy Spirit within? Are you attentive to the voice of your Shepherd? Do you respond obediently as young Samuel did when God called him? He answered without hesitation: "Speak Lord, for Your servant hears."

Have you become so familiar with Christ's character that you are learning to distinguish God's voice, from all the noise and deception in our world that vie for your attention? Today when your Shepherd speaks to you, be willing to act in prompt and cheerful obedience to His voice!

"Dear Shepherd, I thank you for loving me and for tenderly caring for me I purpose to follow You in obedience."

Devotional #25

Security in Christ

Insecurity is a malady that has infected our culture. So many people feel they just never quite measure up. Sadly, the world sets the standard by which most of us measure our appearance, our happiness, our personality, and our degree of success. However, the gospel of salvation has the power to set us free from the comparison trap! Christians can live in the marvelous security of the blessed, finished work of Jesus Christ. Our security grows out of the knowledge that we are accepted in our Beloved Heavenly Father.

Furthermore, we're secure in the realization that we can choose to walk each day in abundant joy and victory. We know our eternal destiny is secure. God gives us countless assurances in His Word that reinforce the wondrous security that is ours.

We are children of God and He assures us that all things work together for our good. He has promised us in Romans 8:38,39 that nothing shall ever separate us from His glorious love—not even death. And He guarantees us that no one can snatch us out of His hand once we belong to Him.

We have been utterly and permanently delivered from the domain of darkness, and transferred to God's kingdom. We are free forever from condemnation. We no longer have to cower in fear, because we've been given a spirit of power, love, and a sound mind. We may approach God with boldness and confidence.

God Himself began a good work in us and we can be certain He will complete that work. Because of His strength in us, we can do all things that are required of us. Almighty God has sealed our salvation with the atoning blood of Christ, and we find in Him, grace and mercy for our every need. Indeed, we are irrevocably and blissfully secure in Christ Jesus.

"Dear Lord, how I praise You that I am securely hidden with Christ in God."

Devotional #26

I am Significant in Christ

Have you noted the tragic sense of personal worthlessness that pervades our world? Everywhere, people frantically try to define their worth in jobs, in designer fashions, in expensive homes, or luxury cars. Yet, they're inevitably frustrated in their quest for significance. Why? Because a person's worth cannot be defined by how smart he is, or what he looks like, or by how much wealth he has amassed.

Countless numbers of people today feel isolated and alienated from their fellow man. A belief that they are insignificant is what drives many people to commit suicide. Their loneliness envelops and overwhelms them. Bereft of hope, they find no compelling reason to go on living.

The truth is that we find our worth in Jesus Christ alone. We are His beloved children and He has chosen us and appointed us to bear fruit. We are His temples on this earth and His Spirit dwells in us. He has entrusted us with a ministry of reconciliation. He appoints us to work diligently as His ambassadors to introduce lost people to God through the person and work of our Savior Jesus Christ.

With the currency of His own shed blood, the Lord has bought us with a price. We are members of Christ's Body. He has given us peace with God and He calls us saints—people set apart for a holy work. The Father created us as His workmanship for good works in this life, and He has granted us eternal citizenship in heaven for the life to come.

He commands us to be the light of the world so the darkness will be illumined. He also intends His children to be the salt of the earth, to act as a preservative in a corrupt and rotting world. We are joined to Him and we are one spirit with Him. We find our sense of worth and identity in no one else.

"Lord God, I thank You that I am significant to You because You created me, and redeemed me with Your Son's perfect blood."

Devotional #27
Unshakable Courage

Are you grounded in Jesus Christ? If you are, nothing can shake your foundation. When your life is anchored on the Rock of your salvation, no difficult relationship, no trial, and no hardship can overwhelm your heart with sorrow.

Is your hope and trust in the Lord? He will not fail you! Consider the words of Ephesians 3:16-18: "And I pray that you, being rooted and established in love, may have power, together with all the saints, to grasp how wide and long and high and deep is the love of Christ."

Be courageous! The Lord has promised to go before you, and He has told you that the battle is not yours. Don't ever be afraid or discouraged, for God is with you. Though troubling circumstances may loom threateningly before you this day, keep a steadfast heart and don't allow the twin thieves of fear and dread to rob you of your quiet confidence in God.

Confidently ask your Heavenly Father for grace to make it through this threatening trial, one day at a time. Resist the temptation to be overwhelmed by the magnitude of this hardship.

Remember that God will keep you in perfect peace when you choose to focus your heart on Him. Refuse to fix your eyes on the difficult circumstances that would draw your loving gaze away from Him. This moment, commit your heart to looking outward.

Above all, don't allow self-pity to consume you. Get out of your circle of sorrow. Find specific ways to demonstrate your love for others. We know that God loves us because Christ laid down His life for us. Likewise, we must lay our lives down in deeds of love, just as our Savior did. Fear and doubt are powerless to lure your unshakable, immoveable heart away from God's agenda for you this day!

"Lord I ask You to make my heart steadfast and immovably rooted in You."

Devotional #28
God Sees Our Hearts

Many people who don't claim the name of Christ are, nonetheless, honest, industrious, friendly, and generous. Even though someone possesses good morals, he has not necessarily "passed from death into life."

Think about the rich young ruler in Matthew 19. He had demonstrated a steady, consistent goodness in his life "from his youth up." He was willing to pursue more information regarding his whole duty in life. He was also a bright young man—he went to the *right* person and he asked the *right* question.

He asked Jesus, "What do I yet lack?" Yet in spite of all of his desirable attributes and the morality he boasted of, he refused to deny himself, take up his cross, and follow Christ. We read that even after receiving the *right* answer, he went *sorrowfully* away.

God tells us in His Word that the human heart is "deceitful above all things and desperately wicked." In our fallen state, we pass judgment on one another's outward appearance. But God penetrates to the depths of our innermost being, and He alone sees our hearts. He judges the quality of our deeds by the disposition of our hearts.

Are you willing to examine your heart before the Lord? Today, invite Him to reveal any impure motives that indwell you and hinder you in your daily walk with Him.

Here are several helpful questions to ask yourself as you undertake this process: Do my words and deeds have their origin in holy motives, or are they prompted by self-interest? Do I strive to bring God glory and further the goals of His Kingdom, or am I motivated by a desire to promote my own agenda and myself? Remember, "good morals" are of no value to the Lord unless they grow out of love and devotion to Him.

"Father, I know it is true that 'as a man thinks in his heart, so he is.' Lord, I ask you to purify my deepest, hidden motives. "

Devotional #29
Loving God's Character

In the Bible the Psalmist cries out: "Who have I in heaven but You? There is none on the earth that I desire besides You." Our Heavenly Father wants us to rest upon Him as our chief happiness. He desires that we seek His good pleasure above the approval and commendation of others.

When we were lost in our sin, we were God's enemies. We took no delight in His excellence and we felt no gratitude for His favors toward us. We may have cried out in terror to Him in the midst of some crisis, hoping that He would intervene on our behalf and rescue us. But our hearts certainly did not adore Him. And we didn't feel any joy in His presence.

Now that we're saved, we praise God because He upholds us, He pardons us, He sanctifies us, and He blesses us. We bow down before Him in thanksgiving because He died in our place so we could pass from death into life. Angels have no cause for this kind of gratitude!

This day, focus on loving God because of Who He is. Ask yourself: Am I pleased with His character and do I love every part of it—His holiness as well as His grace? His justice as well as His mercy? Is there anyone or anything that I love more than God? If so, I am guilty of worshipping an idol and I must repent.

Do I ever spend time meditating on what happiness it will be to live with Him forever in heaven? Do I see inexpressible beauty and glory in almost everything because it is all the work of His hand and because it reflects the excellence of His nature?

As you meditate on God's marvelous, incomparable character, your response can only be a heart full of admiration, gratitude, and joy.

"Father, teach me to love You, not so much because of what You do for me, but because of Who You are."

Devotional #30
Denying Ourselves

In the late 60's, a song emerged on the Christian scene entitled, "They'll Know We Are Christians by Our Love." It became quite popular, and we often held hands as we sang it around a campfire on the beach, as we opened a home Bible study meeting, or as we gathered around the outside of the pews at the end of a worship service.

Love *is* the identifying mark of a Christian. Those who want to love others with the love of Christ must be willing to deny themselves. In every child of God, self-denial should be the prominent distinguishing feature.

Jesus tells us in Matthew 16:24,25: "If any man will come after Me, let him deny himself, take up his cross and follow Me. Whosoever will save his life shall lose it, and whosoever shall lose his life for My sake shall find it."

A Christian learns the spirit of self-denial only as he calmly and deliberately devotes himself to obedience to God, and to the highest good of others. He comes to understand that there is nothing too dear in his life to give to Christ.

He acknowledges that there's nothing too great to be cheerfully sacrificed for the furthering of God's glory. He determines that there's no duty so hard that he is not firmly resolved to perform willingly.

Jesus denied Himself in all that He did, and in all that He suffered. He did not please Himself and He did not seek His own glory. He didn't accumulate riches, He didn't seek prestigious titles—He didn't even have His own home ("a place to lay His head.")

He mission, instead, was to glorify His Father Who sent Him. He came to earth not to be served, but to serve. Until we reach heaven, we will never achieve such a state of pure self-denial, unmixed with any selfishness.

The goal toward which we must strive, however, is clearly stated for us in 2 Corinthians 5:15: "He died for all that they who live should not henceforth live unto themselves, but unto Him who died for them and rose again."

Today, ask God to subdue your selfish tendencies and to give you opportunities to deny yourself for His sake.

"Lord please teach me to live not unto myself, but unto You so You will be glorified."

Devotional #31
Examine Yourselves

God declares in His Word that all of mankind is vile enough to make it necessary for the Son of God to die for their salvation. The Redeemed of the ages will have all of eternity to thank the Lord Jesus for His ultimate sacrifice on their behalf.

Most Christians can wholeheartedly cry out with the beggar, in the book of Matthew: "Whereas once I was blind, now I see." Yet, lest we forget our hopelessness and helplessness apart from Christ, we are instructed in 2 Corinthians 13:5: "Examine yourselves to see if you are in the faith."

Several questions are helpful as you initiate this self-examination: Do I give up easily when I encounter trials and difficulties, or do I persevere in running the race of my Christian life, so I will obtain the prize of Christ Jesus? Do I stay focused on specific spiritual goals to fight the good fight with certainty, and not as one who vainly "beats the air?"

Am I building my life on shifting sand and on things that will pass away, or am I anchored on Jesus Christ, the Rock? Am I puffed up with a sense of my own importance? Do I pursue knowledge alone, believing the widespread deception that "I am what I know?" Am I mindful that throughout the ages, many people have tragically gone down to eternal damnation, replete with knowledge of God and His Son? Do I take heed of the truth that even the demons tremble at Jesus' name?

Do I seek godly wisdom by spending time each day in prayer and reading His Word? Do I set aside time to praise and worship Him on a regular basis? Do I steward my time and my possessions in a way that pleases my Heavenly Father?

God wants His children to walk in a manner worthy of their calling. Ask Him this day, to grant you the grace to press on faithfully, toward the mark of the upward call in Christ Jesus.

"Father, God, please guard me from fainthearted faith, and cause me to run Your race without growing weary."

Devotional #32

Loving God for Who He Is

The writer of Matthew 10:37 reminds us that God does not accept a divided heart: "He that loves father or mother more than Me is not worthy of Me." When we consider the fact that God pardons our sin, reconciles us to Himself, and sanctifies us in His Truth, we ought to cry out to Him in loving gratitude.

When we reflect upon His faithfulness to uphold us throughout our years, to protect us from the schemes of the Enemy, and to bless us daily with abundance and goodness, our hearts should overflow with thanksgiving.

Our goal, as faithful children of God, is to learn to delight in Him *not* for what He does for us, but for Who He is. We can rest in the certainty that He never changes and His purity is unblemished. We can be confident of the fact that while His goodness is universal, His justice is inflexible. He is a God of perfect holiness and infinite grace.

What exactly is meant by the statement that God is a jealous God? Simply this: He *must* be the primary object of our affection. Thus, there are certain questions that a Christian should regularly ask himself: Do I love God more than I love anyone else? Is there anyone I prefer spending time with?

Do I love Him when He disciplines me? Do I recall with genuine grief, my life of sin before He saved me? Do I truly believe this world is not my home? Am I thrilled by the knowledge that one day I will behold Him face to face—and spend eternity with Him and be perfected by Him?

Today, cry out in thanksgiving to God as you remember your mountain of transgressions that He has so graciously and gloriously forgiven. Throughout this day, dwell on God's holy character and take time to tell Him *why* you love Him.

"Dear Lord, teach me to love and adore You in a way that pleases You supremely."

Devotional #33

Godly Sorrow vs. Worldly Sorrow

King Saul, Esau, and Judas all had something in common. All three men were guilty of ungodly repentance. Like a child who trembles in dread of impending punishment, they were sorry that "their sins had found them out." They lamented the personal loss and embarrassment they endured because of their sins. They did not, however, express authentic remorse to God for the vileness of their sins.

The writer of Proverbs 28:13 declares: "Whoever covers his sins shall not prosper, but whoever confesses and forsakes them shall find mercy." An essential ingredient in true repentance is changed behavior—a willingness to walk in the opposite direction—*away* from your sin. Where there is no forsaking of sin, there can be no genuine repentance.

Several key questions help us determine whether we are demonstrating real, godly sorrow when we repent before God for our sins: Do I truly hate the sin I have committed, or do I fear punishment and the awful accompanying feelings of guilt? Do I mourn over my sin because I've shamed myself, or because I have offended God's holiness?

When I come before God in prayer and get a fresh picture of my vain thoughts, my unfaithfulness, and my ingratitude, am I mindful that apart from Christ, I am forever ruined?

Am I grieved because I am proud, self-centered, and worldly, or do I try to "dress-up" and excuse my offenses? Do I ever minimize the seriousness of my sin? Am I willing to make any sacrifice necessary, to be delivered from my sin?

Ask the Lord this day to cause your conscience to grow increasingly tender toward the Holy Spirit's promptings each time you're tempted to go astray. Be quick to confess and repent of your sins whenever God's Spirit convicts you.

"Dear God, cause me to repent in godly sorrow. According to Your mercy, I ask You to keep sin far from me."

Devotional #34
Saved by Grace

Christians should take great comfort in Ephesians 2:8,9: "For by grace you have been saved through faith; and that not of yourselves, it is the gift of God; not as a result of works that no one should boast." Faith is reliance upon the immutable testimony of God's Word.

Many Christians vividly recall the time when the Holy Spirit first revealed to them the awareness that they had sinned against a Holy God. They had a keen sense of their fallen, guilty state, and they understood that in their condemned condition, they were at the mercy of God, whom they had offended. They may have realized, as well, that God was under no obligation to save them from the destruction they so rightly deserved.

Most Believers also remember understanding, for the first time ever, the glorious truth that *all* their former good deeds they had once relied upon, no longer offered them any hope.

They cast themselves exclusively upon Jesus Christ and His redeeming grace—God's only appointed means for saving sinners. They no longer rejected the cross as a stumbling block, but gloried in Jesus' cross, and happily committed themselves to faith in Christ alone.

Have you relinquished all the things that were once "gain" to you, and counted them "loss" for Christ Jesus? Do you view everything that you are and everything that you have as "nothing," in order to win Christ? Do you long to be found in Him, not having your own righteousness, but instead, having a righteousness that is achieved through faith in Christ from God Himself?

Yield yourself to Jesus as a full and complete Savior. Thank Him that you are saved by His death, governed by His laws, protected by His power, and sanctified by His Holy Spirit.

"Lord I surrender every aspect of my life to You. I am Yours, to be used for Your pleasure and to promote Your glory."

Devotional #35

The Command of Humility

The Bible clearly depicts the natural state of man as independent, haughty, and proud. Christians can be grateful to God that He faithfully works in His children's lives to subdue this spirit of pride.

When God grants us the insight that we are utterly dependent upon Him, we become aware of our unworthiness. We identify with the cry of the prodigal son in Luke 15:21 when he returned home: "Father, I have sinned against heaven and in your sight, and am no more worthy to be called your son."

We begin to perceive the truth of Lamentations 3:22: "It is of the Lord's *mercies* that I am not consumed." We embrace wholeheartedly, God's *justice* that would condemn us, were it not for His enduring mercy. And we admire and adore His *graciousness* that rescues us from certain condemnation.

Are you careful *not* to think more highly of yourself than you ought? Do you practice ministering to others' needs before you attend to your own needs?

Ask the Lord to examine your heart and reveal to you the pride and vanity that reside there. The Holy Spirit will be faithful to show you when your love "is puffed up and when it behaves unbecomingly." He will lovingly discipline you when you seek the praise of men, more than the praise of God. He will grant you an increasing desire to remain humble until the end of your days.

Be ever mindful of the fact that the pride in your heart constantly distorts your view of your true character. It causes you to attempt to conceal your sin from God and from your fellow man. Strive toward the goal for Christ-like humility, as stated in Philippians 2:3: "Do nothing from selfishness or empty conceit, but with humility of mind let each one of you regard one another as more important than himself."

"Dear Father, keep me mindful of my unworthiness and of Your perfect sufficiency for all my needs."

Devotional #36
Accounting for Our Time

One of my favorite poems has just two lines: "Only one life, it will soon be passed. Only what's done for Christ will last." A Christian must think about this question daily: "How can I most successfully accomplish my Master's work, every hour of every day that I'm allowed to live on this earth?"

For the child of God, there is no division of time into the *secular* and the *sacred*. All time is consecrated to God. Every Believer should be thoroughly convinced that he will one day give an account to God for how wisely or foolishly he stewarded his allotted time during this life.

Since we know from Scripture that Jesus Christ "went about doing good," we can conclude that God is well pleased when we actively seek the good of others. The writer of John 15:8 exhorts us: "Herein is My Father glorified, that you bear much fruit, so shall you be My disciples."

Christians who remain aware of their absolute dependence upon God, delight in utilizing their time on earth to serve and glorify their Redeemer. They derive great joy from doing good deeds for their fellow man.

No child of God can be truly content being habitually idle, or wasting his time in empty pursuits and vain amusements. Begin to determine, for example, whether you attend social events merely for enjoyment, or to "make Christ known" to others. Do you read only for pleasure, or also to be challenged in your walk with the Lord?

Examine whether you consume great blocks of time reading novels, watching movies, TV shows, or sports. Commit *all* your time to the Lord, to be used however He deems best. Ask God today to help you find your highest happiness in devoted duty to Him.

"Lord Jesus, I long to redeem the time that I have carelessly squandered. I dedicate every remaining day of my life to honoring and glorifying You."

Devotional #37

The Necessity of Prayer

Someone has beautifully described prayer as "the Christian's breath." To live without prayer is to live without God in our lives. There is no such thing as a Christian who does not pray.

We find, however, in Mark 7:6 that there is such a thing as "drawing near to God with the mouth and honoring Him with the lips, while the heart is far from Him." This kind of prayer is nothing more than a useless formality, and it dishonors the Lord.

As we study Scripture, we understand that God will not accept a prayer that is not sincere and humble. We see a marvelous example of humility as we read about the publican described in Luke 18:13. He would not even lift his eyes to heaven, but beat his breast crying, "God, be merciful to me, a sinner."

We find a similar passage in the Old Testament, in Ezra 9:6: "Oh my God, I am ashamed, and blush to lift up my face to You. For our iniquities have multiplied over our heads, and our guilt has grown even to the heavens."

God's Word assures us that we can fully believe His promises when we pray to Him. Although we have a sense of personal unworthiness, we know that we have a great High Priest, Jesus Christ, who hears our every prayerful utterance.

The writer of Hebrews 4:15 tells us that Jesus is sympathetic to our weaknesses because He was tempted in all things, as we are tempted. Yet He lived a perfect life without sin. Scripture gloriously exhorts us: "Draw near with confidence to the throne of grace, that you may receive mercy and find grace to help in time of need."

Do you mutter a few sentences of meaningless prayer each day, or has God's Spirit taught you to pray because you are weak and need power? Today, confess to God that you are tempted and you need His strength and His support.

Admit that you are a sinner who needs mercy. Tell Him you are in want and you need supply. He invites you to come to Him with every need, no matter how small or seemingly insignificant. God is your Great Shepherd, and His loving-kindness is better than life.

"O Lord, let me not neglect the practice of secret prayer. Teach me to live in a moment-by-moment awareness that every breath I take depends upon Your grace alone."

Devotional #38
Do You Love the Brethren?

A primary evidence of someone's salvation is whether or not he demonstrates genuine love for his brothers and sisters in Christ. The writer of John 13:34 declares: "I give you a new commandment, that you love one another." We find this directive restated in 1 John 3:23: "And this is His commandment, that we should believe on His Son Jesus Christ, and love one another."

When we have a spirit of brotherly love, we bless those who curse us, and we do good deeds for those who hate us. God's Word instructs us to do good to all men, but *especially* to those of the household of faith. There is a particularly fervent love that is reserved for fellow followers of Christ.

Something in the character of every child of God reflects the image of his heavenly Father. We share the same convictions and we hold fast to the same hopes. We do battle together against the same spiritual enemies, and we labor under the same discouragements.

We understand the temptations that we must all resist in order to obey our Lord, and we look forward to spending eternity together in heaven. It's no wonder, then, that we should love one another sincerely and with a pure heart. We have a solid foundation for mutual friendship because of our eternal bond in Jesus Christ.

Do you love your brothers and sisters in Christ even when they disappoint you? Do you bear with their weaknesses, and pray for them and watch over them? Do you rejoice when they rejoice, weep when they weep, and gladly bear their burdens as your own? How about when they rebuke you?

According to John 13:35, the world judges the sincerity of our faith by our love for the brethren: "By this shall all men know that you are my disciples, if you love one another."

"Dear God, teach me to love my brothers and sisters in Christ with a selfless and unconditional love."

Devotional #39
Living a Separated Life

As followers of Jesus Christ, if we believe Hebrews 11:13,14, we should be convinced that we are strangers and exiles on this earth. We will never feel truly "at home" until we reach heaven. For there, is where our treasures lie.

All around us, we can observe ample evidence that the spirit of this world is pride and self-indulgence—not humility or self-denial. The world pursues pleasures, riches, and honor, and frequently makes a general mockery of holy pursuits. Christians love what the world despises, and the world chases after those things from which Christians are commanded to flee.

In order to live a separated life, you must acknowledge the fact that you are a pilgrim and a foreigner—passing through this life on the narrow way that leads to your eternal home in heaven. Do you view this world through the eyes of faith? Do you ask God for strength to "be in the world but not of it?" As you think of the world in light of eternity, do you glory in the blessed hope of the cross of Jesus Christ? The same cross that is foolishness to the world is life to us who have been delivered from the dominion of darkness.

Unrepentant sinners are traveling the broad path that leads to death. Yet we must not self-righteously close ourselves off from the world. God commands us to build relationships with unbelievers so we will have opportunities to reach out to them with Christ's love, and minister to their needs.

We ought to have compassion on them and respect them as fellow members of society. We should earnestly and lovingly attempt to share the gospel with them. Their tragic destiny, apart from Christ, is to be pitied. While we reach out to them with the message of salvation, we need to remain mindful of the truth of James 4:4: "Friendship with the world is enmity with God."

"Heavenly Father, remind me of the truths of Your Word, that this world is not my home, and that light has no fellowship with darkness."

Devotional #40
Love Not the World

We read a piercing question in Amos 3:3: "How can two walk together unless they be agreed?" Until a lost man repents of his sin and cries out to God for salvation, there is an irreconcilable spirit between him and a follower of Christ.

The foremost desire of a Christian is to obey God. He reverently fears God more than he fears his fellow man. He refuses to dishonor God in an effort to please people. He understands that he cannot court the intimate friendship of unregenerate people because he has a clear admonition in Scripture against such an alliance. We read this stern warning in 1 Corinthians 15:33: "Do not be misled: 'Bad company corrupts good character.' " Believers must not ignore this caveat!

When we fix our highest affections on human relationships, wealth, fame, and sensual pleasures, we cannot fix them supremely on God. Jesus tells us that no one can serve two masters. We will invariably love one and hate the other.

For the Christian who wants to determine whether or not he is being conformed to this world, several questions are pertinent: Do I imitate the examples of the world, or have I set my affections on things above? Do I shrink from certain Christian duties, such as witnessing, or reading my Bible in a public place, because that would be unpopular? Do I pursue friendships with the "rich and honorable" more than with the most humble brother or sister in Christ? Are any of my closest friendships with unbelievers?

The writer of 1 John 2:15 exposes the futility of double-mindedness: "If any man loves the world, the love of the Father is not in him." Today, be encouraged and warned by the words of Proverbs 13:20: "He that walks with wise men shall be wise. But a companion of fools shall be destroyed."

"Lord God, I know that this world will one day pass away. I desire to set my foremost affections on You and on eternal things above."

Devotional #41
Pressing On

In Psalm 1, the Psalmist compares the spiritual growth of a Christian to a tree that thrives in good, well-watered soil. "And he shall be like a tree, firmly planted by streams of water, which yields its fruit in its season, and its leaf shall not wither, and in whatever he does, he prospers."

The writer of 1 Peter 2:2 likens young converts to "newborn *babes,* who long for the pure milk of the Word." We should not, however, remain in a spiritually infantile state. In Ephesians 4:14, Paul admonishes us to "no longer be *children,* foolishly tossed to and fro by every wind of false doctrine."

Instead, God commands us to grow up to be *mature men and women* of faith, and attain the full stature of Christ. We can only accomplish this by persevering in faith—by "pressing on" in the face of hardships.

God grants His covenant grace to every Believer, to support him through every step of his pilgrimage. He has promised His children in Philippians 1:6 that when He begins a good work in an individual's life, He will faithfully complete it.

A true Christian understands that conversion is only the first step of a spiritual journey. We do not consider ourselves as having "arrived." The more we recognize and acknowledge our own sins, the more we delight in God's holy character. As God progressively empties us of ourselves, we have a greater desire to rest upon Christ as our only hope. The more we grow to love God, the deeper our longing is to know and love Him more fully.

As we fulfill our Christian duties, we find increasing joy in performing them. The more we encounter trials and difficulties, the more determined we are to persevere to the end. Isaiah 40:29 is a glorious promise for every Christian: "He gives power to the faint, and to them that have no might, He increases strength."

"Dear Lord, I wait upon You to renew my strength to press on in faith to the end of my journey."

Devotional #42
Aim for the Prize

As people of God grow in grace, they begin to have less confidence in their own feeble strength and an increasing awareness of their utter dependence upon God. They have experienced the grief and folly of trusting in themselves.

They are progressively more patient when they encounter suffering. And they are more likely to point out the strengths of others rather than their weaknesses, for fear of judging them—something Matthew 7:1 strictly forbids.

They grow more adept at controlling their emotions and they learn to apply Proverbs 14:29 to their daily lives: "He who is slow to anger has great understanding." While young Christians often neglect their commitments to God and their fellow man, more mature Christians learn to carry out their responsibilities in a timely and cheerful manner.

Perhaps the most visible sign of spiritual growth in a Believer's life is the consistent character and peaceful calm that seem to radiate from his life. Although he *runs the race* and *fights the fight*, as Scripture commands him to do, he focuses on the prize of Christ Jesus. Despite the inevitable moments of doubt and weariness, he makes measurable progress forward from "glory to glory."

Growth in grace, however, is not always forward-moving. We wander away from the narrow path, and become discouraged and distracted. Sometimes we actually move backwards for a season.

Yet we must unfailingly aim at the "crown of righteousness which fades not away." The clearest manifestation of godly character is to continue pressing forward—refusing to give up. We should never allow ourselves to feel satisfied with our present state.

God commands us to work out our salvation in fear and trembling. We know that works do not save us. Only the shed blood of Jesus Christ atones for our sin. But each time we find ourselves beginning to live like a spiritual sluggard, making no new advances in faith, we should soberly heed the warning of 2 Corinthians 13:5: "Examine yourselves, therefore, whether you be in the faith."

"I beseech You, Lord, to give me the strength and determination never to give up in my Christian pilgrimage."

Devotional #43
He Is Touched with Our Frailties

Many of us witness the towering faith and impressive accomplishments of other Christians, and we feel like a weak and powerless child of God in comparison. Yet we should be encouraged by the words of Isaiah 42:3: "A bruised reed He will not break, and a dimly burning wick He will not extinguish."

Jesus is our advocate and an ever-present help in time of need. The fullness of the Godhead bodily dwells in Him, and we are hidden with Christ in God. He is acquainted with our sorrows, and He is our hope and our comfort. God appointed Him as the One Who would bear our grief and carry our burdens. He heals the broken-hearted and comforts those who mourn. He invites us to cast every care on Him.

Christ is fully sufficient for our every need. When we must engage in spiritual warfare, He is our Buckler and our Shield. When we lack understanding and discernment, He is our Wisdom. When Satan accuses us, He is our Advocate, our Righteousness and our Defense.

When our way is not clear, He is the Light for our path. When we feel unprofitable as a servant in God's kingdom, we recall with joy, that He is our Sanctification. We take great comfort in the gentle reminder of Psalm 103:14: "He knows our frame and remembers that we are but dust."

Jesus is our tender Shepherd who, as Isaiah 40:11 beautifully explains, "will gather the lambs in His arms, and carry them in His bosom and gently lead those that are with young." There can be no higher delight, and no greater privilege than to consecrate yourself completely to Christ Jesus who died for you. Surrender to Him who is seated at God's right hand, and who ever lives to make intercession for you.

"Thank You, loving Father, that You have rooted and established me in Jesus Christ the Lord. My heart abounds with gratitude and thanksgiving."

Devotional #44

God is My Desire

If asked whether or not they worship idols, most Christians would adamantly respond that they do not! What Believer doesn't know of God's warning to His children in the Ten Commandments, *not* to have any other Gods before Him, and *not* to make any idols to worship?

The sad truth, however, is this: idols abound in the hearts of most followers of Christ. An idol is defined as anything or anyone that we want more than we want Jesus Christ in our lives. God demands the undivided devotion of our hearts, and He wants to be our greatest refuge in times of need.

When our goal, for example, is to achieve personal happiness, we are pursuing an idol. Our primary goal in life should be to please God. Jesus teaches us in Matthew 22:37 that the greatest commandment in the Law is this: "You shall love the Lord your God with all your heart, and with all your soul, and with all your mind." God will not accept a divided heart.

The degree of joy that you experience each day depends upon what you have your heart *set* on. Pray regularly, that the Lord will give you godly motives, and that He will build contentment into your life, regardless of how difficult your circumstances may be.

Are you dealing with unhappiness in your Christian walk because you're guilty of the sin of idolatry? The Enemy of your faith will attempt to blind you to this possibility. Yet if you want anything or anyone more than you want God, you are indeed, worshipping an idol.

What is your heart set on? Whom do you love the most? Do you hunger and thirst for God, as a deer pants for the water? Have you truthfully determined and admitted to God the things and relationships that are most important to you?

If you've realized you are guilty of the sin of idolatry, confess it to the Lord and repent of it. Begin now to thank God for your present circumstances. Have faith that He will glorify Himself through your life, as you worship Him alone.

"O God, keep my mind stayed on You and restrain me from following after idols."

Devotional #45
Greeting God Joyfully

When you were a child, did your parents ever ask you if you had "gotten up on the wrong side of the bed?" Some people seem to awaken with a sunny disposition, ready to face the world with a smile and an encouraging word.

There are other people, however, who are not so pleasant. Fellow family members tend to cut a wide path around their morning grumpiness.

How do you greet the Lord each morning? The Psalmist tells God in Psalm 5:3: "In the morning, O Lord, You will hear my voice. I will order my prayer to You and eagerly watch."

The great Christian leader, George Mueller, suggested that the best plan for starting our day successfully is to seek God's face before we see anyone else's face, and to hear God's voice before we hear the voice of man.

This means you must get alone with God and praise Him for the privilege of another day of life. Spend time thanking Him specifically for His many blessings. Singing hymns and praise choruses aloud to Him is an amazing way to "jump start" your morning. (It's always easier to "act" yourself into a new way of feeling, than it is to "feel" yourself into a new way of acting!)

Remember that God doesn't *owe* us anything. A fresh, new day is a profound gift from His hand. We should never take a single day for granted. We would do well to make the words of Psalm 118:24 our own: "This is the day that the Lord has made. I *will* rejoice and be glad in it." I "will" means I "choose to."

By the way, one key ingredient for waking up with a heart of praise is to be sure you don't let the sun to set on your anger the previous evening. Strive to keep all your relationships current. Ask forgiveness from anyone you've offended, and you will sleep more peacefully. Then rejoice that His mercies are new every morning.

"Lord, as for me, I will joyfully sing of Your loving-kindness in the morning."

Devotional #46
The Second Mile

The writer of Hebrews 12:15 commands us: "See to it that no one comes short of the grace of God, that no root of bitterness springing up causes trouble, and by it, many be defiled." When we disobey the directive of 1 Corinthians 13:5, and choose to keep an account of wrongs suffered, we run the risk of becoming bitter.

In our bitterness, we nurse our grudge and replay it over repeatedly in our minds. We begin to believe that we are innocent victims, and our bitterness becomes contagious. As we rehearse our hurts, first with one person, then another, we poison and defile them with gossip and bitter words. This is where the "second mile" principle comes into play!

Have you ever wondered about the meaning of Jesus' words in Matthew 5:41 when He says, "And whoever shall force you to go one mile, go with him two?" The Jews were often bitter toward the Roman government for imposing many strict laws upon their nation. One of these laws stated that a Roman soldier could require a Jew to carry his pack for the distance of one mile in any direction.

A Jew who complied with the law and resentfully carried a soldier's pack for one mile, did nothing more than discharge his legal duty. However, he could demonstrate to the soldier his love for God, by volunteering to do more than was required of him. Jesus taught the principle of going the second mile because He was well acquainted with the corrupt heart of man.

Paul instructs us in Romans 12:21: "Do not be overcome by evil, but overcome evil with good." When someone wrongs us, we gain spiritual freedom from bitterness by investing something of value in the evildoer's life. Ask God today, to reveal to you any secret bitterness that you may be harboring in your heart. Repent of it and find a way to do a good deed for the person who hurt you.

"Father, God, please teach me how to go the second mile, and make me a blessing to my enemies."

Devotional #47

The Names of God

It is a marvelous and enlightening pursuit to consider the many different names of God. Our Heavenly Father has chosen to reveal Himself to us through His various names that are recorded in the Bible. We encounter five very important names of God in the book of Genesis.

God introduces Himself in Genesis 1:1 as **Elohim**. "In the beginning God created the heavens and the earth." This name speaks of plurality and establishes the fact that God has always been a triune God. It also refers to His mighty power, His authority, and His majesty. The words of Genesis 1:26 reinforce the doctrine of the Trinity: "God said, 'Let *Us* make man in *Our* image, according to *Our* likeness.'"

We meet **Jehovah**, "our eternal God," in Genesis 2:7. "Jehovah" signifies covenant relationship, without which, we cannot worship Him. **El Shaddai**, "God our Supplier," appears in Genesis 17:1,2, when He promises Abraham a son. This name describes God's bountiful blessings.

We discover a beautiful name of God, **Adonai**, in Genesis 18:3, when God explains to Abraham what His plans are for Sodom and Gomorrah. This name represents God's ownership and Lordship over our lives.

Jehovah-Jireh, "God, my Provider," reveals Himself in Genesis 22:14, when Abraham is about to offer his son Isaac up as a sacrifice in obedience to God. God stops him and provides a ram as a substitute offering.

This moving story is a foreshadowing of the ultimate sacrifice that would be made generations later by the Lamb of God, Jesus Christ, on the cross. God, in His mercy, provides for our salvation and He supplies all we need each day to live and to glorify Him.

"Dear Lord, may I come to know and cherish every aspect of Your holy character, as revealed through Your many powerful names."

Devotional #48

Love is Patient and Kind

The goal of every Christian should be to love others with the kind of love described in 1 Corinthians 13. No matter how gifted we may be, until we master this kind of love, we appear to our heavenly Father as a "noisy gong or a clanging symbol."

Love is patient. This does not mean that we are to be patient only when we *feel* like being patient. The writer of 1 Thessalonians 5:18 exhorts us to "give thanks in everything."

We can choose to be patient in the midst of a situation where tension is building, by thanking God for each irritating detail. God will use every trying incident that occurs to mold our character for godliness, if we don't resist His training.

Love is kind. We find a powerful statement of how highly God values the virtue of kindness in Romans 2:4: "Do you think lightly of the riches of His kindness and forbearance, and patience, not knowing that the kindness of God leads you to repentance?"

God demonstrated the ultimate act of kindness, in that while we were yet sinners, He sent His Son to the cross to die for our sins. We demonstrate kindness to others by performing kind deeds for them and by maintaining a gentle tone of voice.

Harsh, critical Christians drive other people away, while kind-hearted Christians draw people to Jesus Christ and to themselves, opening boundless opportunities for ministry.

Love is not jealous. Jealous people are wrapped up in themselves. Insecure and fearful, they live in dread of being displaced by someone or something, and they are focused primarily on their own wants and needs.

A loving person considers other people as more important than himself and is, therefore, focused on the needs and desires of others.

Today, ask the Lord to give you opportunities to act patiently and kindly toward those you come in contact with. Pray that you will focus your love and energies on others—not on yourself.

"Lord, please convict me when I am being impatient, jealous, or unkind. Teach me to love people as You love them."

Devotional #49

Love is Not Arrogant or Rude

Consider the exhortation we find in 2 Corinthians 10:17,18: "He who boasts, let him boast in the Lord. For he who commends himself is not approved, but whom the Lord commends is approved." God's Word warns us that *love does not brag*. People who boast about themselves have an inflated appreciation of their worth, and they are usually attempting to make themselves look better than they really are. The writer of Proverbs reminds us to let someone else's lips commend us, and not our own.

Love is not arrogant. An arrogant person is full of self-importance. Most of us have been acquainted at some point in our lives with a "know-it-all." A know-it-all is someone who's very opinionated about any subject that comes up, and he becomes defensive and hostile when challenged or corrected on a particular point. He generally doesn't allow those people closest to him to have their own opinions, insisting that others agree with him on everything.

God wants His children to be humble and servant-hearted, putting others before themselves. Believers should be willing to listen attentively to other peoples' opinions and reproofs. They should remain open to the possibility that they could be wrong about some things. God explains in the book of Proverbs that a fool hates the person that rebukes him, but a wise man loves someone who cares enough to help him live a more obedient Christian life, by confronting him in love.

Are you excessively aware of your own accomplishments and strengths? Do you sometimes try to impress other people? Are you receptive to the reproofs of others? Do you have a tendency to express your opinions in a dogmatic way? Ask the Lord, today, to humble you and teach you to listen carefully and lovingly to other people.

"Father, I want to reflect the meekness of Christ in my daily walk. Convict me of any arrogance in my heart. I ask that I would decrease and You would increase in my life every day."

Devotional #50

Love Has Good Manners

Love does not act unbecomingly. When we behave rudely and disrespectfully toward someone, we do not reflect the love of Christ. We read in the New Testament that Jesus' character was always consistent. People felt free to approach Him and they never had to "walk on eggshells," for fear that He might be in a sour mood. They could accurately predict that He would be warm and receptive toward them.

Love rejoices in truth and believes all things. The Bible instructs Christians to speak the truth in love. Truth that is spoken without love and grace is harshness. However, love devoid of truth is sentimentality.

Under the guise of loving someone, we often ignore recurring sin in the lives of family members and friends. We thereby enable them to live in disobedience to God. If we truly love someone, we will try to restore him to a right relationship with God.

An important part of loving a person biblically is, by faith, believing the best in him. As we prayerfully entrust him to God's sovereign care, we can be confident that the Lord always works all things together for good in His children's lives.

Ask the Lord today, to cultivate in you a respectful attitude that honors your fellow Believers as image-bearers of God. Consider how you might fulfill the command of Hebrews 10:24, to "stimulate others to love and good deeds."

Commit yourself to the task of speaking wholesome, edifying words in a gentle tone of voice, with a pleasant countenance. Make yourself available to God to help restore disobedient brothers and sisters to a right relationship with Him.

"Gracious heavenly Father, may my love never fail. Teach me how to speak the truth in love. I sincerely want to put away childish things and love others with Your perfect love."

Devotional #51

A Wise Appeal

Is there an authority figure in your life, perhaps a parent, an employer, or a husband, who you think should reconsider a directive or an instruction he has given? Would you like for him to reevaluate a decision he's made? You have biblical recourse in the form of a godly appeal.

Let's examine an appeal made by Daniel, in Daniel 1:8: "Daniel made up his mind that he would not defile himself with the king's food or wine, so he sought *permission* from the commander of the officials that he might not defile himself."

He appealed to his overseer with an alternative plan to be tested for ten days on a diet of vegetables and water. The tone of his appeal was not manipulative, harsh, or disrespectful. And he did not rebelliously demand his own way.

Once you determine the "back-up" plan that you will recommend in your appeal, it's important to decide on the proper time to make the appeal. Make your request only once so you won't be guilty of nagging, or of being contentious and argumentative. If your authority figure is a Christian, it's a good idea to use pertinent Bible verses to reinforce your appeal.

Commit to God ahead of time that you will be willing to do whatever your authority decides, as long as you're not asked to violate Scripture in order to fulfill your authority's wishes. Leave the results in God's hands.

Accept the final decision as God's will for your life at this time. You can make your appeal again at a later time. However, for now, trust the Lord to accomplish His work in your life, regardless of the outcome of your appeal.

"Lord, I ask Your Holy Spirit to lead me to make wise and gentle appeals to those people in authority over me."

Devotional #52
God-Honoring Speech

The Bible teaches us that God takes the matter of our speech very seriously. We demonstrate our reverence for the Lord in the way we speak. The writer of Colossians 4:6 instructs us: "Let your speech always be with grace, seasoned, as it were, with salt, so that you may know how you should respond to each person."

Our culture is infected with an epidemic of foul speech. We can hardly go anywhere today without hearing offensive, irreverent language. We can scarcely make a trip to the grocery store, a restaurant, a public park, or an entertainment event without being subjected to vile obscenities.

We should always be mindful, as Christians, that God is holy and omnipotent. Every small infraction matters to Him. He commands us to live a separated and distinctive lifestyle.

Our speech powerfully sets us apart, or conversely, identifies us with people who defile with their lips. Garbage talk is not something we do accidentally. We consciously choose the words we speak.

A Christian may protest, "I hear so much filthy language at work, or at school, that I can't help it when something 'slips out.'" God, however, never winks at sin. We have complete control over our choices, and we must never be guilty of condoning sinful behavior.

We will not dare to stand before His Judgment Throne and excuse our sin by blaming other people's wrong influences. On that day, God will require each of to give an account of "every idle and careless" word we've ever spoken.

We find a strong warning in James 3:9,10: "With our tongue we bless our Lord and Father; and with it we curse men, who have been made in the likeness of God. From the same mouth come both blessing and cursing. My brethren, these things ought not to be this way."

For a Christian, foul language, and distasteful euphemisms ("substitute" curse words) are *never* acceptable, under any circumstance. Offensive language is destructive, defiling, and sinful. Today, ask God to grant you the grace to speak, at all times, with the dignity of Jesus Christ—in a way that honors Him.

"Dear Father, I repent of my unwholesome, sinful speech and I commit my lips to You, to speak only words that are edifying and healing."

Devotional #53

Spiritual Multiplication

Don had been saved for only one week when he joined a group of high school students on an evangelism mission trip. They hit the beaches, armed with boxes of gospel tracts and hearts full of expectant faith.

They had been equipped with about two hours of training in how to share their faith with unbelievers. He describes it as an experience he will never forget. Don firmly believes that some genuine conversions occurred because of that fledgling, yet earnest endeavor to "make Jesus Christ known."

Don was drawn to Christ because a group of young men in his community had taken seriously the exhortation found in 1 Thessalonians 2:8: "Having thus a fond affection for you, we were well-pleased to impart to you not only the gospel of God but also our own lives."

These men told Don the good news of salvation, and then they spent time with him on a regular basis, teaching him how to apply God's Word to his daily life. They prayed with him, and for him, and they allowed him to accompany them as they went about ministering to people. They encouraged him to be a bold witness for Christ by giving him opportunities to minister under their supervision. They called the process "spiritual multiplication."

The writer of 2 Timothy 2:2 exhorts us: "The things which you have heard from me in the presence of many witnesses, these entrust to faithful men, who will be able to teach others also." Are you regularly teaching the precious truths of Scripture to people who will in turn, teach others?

Ask God, this day, to lead you to someone who desperately needs to be nurtured in the faith. Trust the Lord for the strength, the time, and the wisdom to obey the command of 2 Timothy 2:2.

"Oh Lord, please use me to teach other Christians to 'observe all things that You have commanded.' "

Devotional #54

Surrendering to God's Discipline

In 1 Corinthians 4:2 Paul straightforwardly states: "It is required of stewards that a man be found faithful." God tests our faithfulness by entrusting His agenda to us. He gives us opportunities to minister, and to demonstrate our worthiness as a steward of that which He has entrusted.

We read this truth in Luke 16:10: "Whoever can be trusted with very little can also be trusted with much." As we grow in grace and seek to be consistently faithful and obedient, God often assigns us greater responsibilities in His kingdom.

As we progress in our spiritual journey, God trains us for our tasks by lovingly disciplining us when we are foolish and disobedient. We find these words in Hebrews 12:11: "All discipline for the moment seems not to be joyful, but sorrowful; yet to those who have been trained by it, afterwards it yields the peaceful fruit of righteousness." The purpose of God's discipline is to conform us to His image, and to make us fit for His service.

God admonishes us in His Word to endure the discipline of the Lord because He is treating us as sons. The writer of Hebrews 12:7 asks: "What son is there, whom his father does not discipline?" It is when we do not experience God's discipline that we should be alarmed, for then we are, as the Bible describes it, illegitimate children and *not* sons.

Are you guilty of shrinking from God's hand of discipline? Do you question His love for you when He chastises you? Make a commitment to the Lord, this day, to submit to His perfect plan of disciplining you as His child.

"Father, I praise You for loving me enough to discipline me. I know that You have my best interests in mind, and I submit to Your purposes."

Devotional #55
The Bond of Unity

Satan delights in working confusion and division among the people of God. The Psalmist declares in Psalm 133:1, "Behold how good and pleasant it is for brothers to dwell together in unity." Christians should attempt to live together harmoniously. Unity among the brethren, however, is often difficult to preserve because we are all sinners, and because we are all very different in our temperaments and preferences.

When you encounter conflict with another Believer, are you ever tempted to think self-serving thoughts like these? "There's no hope for resolving this issue. He's a stubborn mule and he's never going to change." Or, "She's so wrapped up in herself she probably won't even listen to what I have to say."

Instead, you ought to ask God what He desires to teach you in the midst of the conflict, and petition Him for the grace and wisdom to resolve the problem in a rational and loving manner. Always begin by searching your heart for any wrong you're responsible for. Then go to the offended person in a spirit of humility and ask forgiveness for your part of the blame. Don't wait for the other person involved to make the first move.

God knows that discord and disunity are like cancers that spread quickly within the body of Christ, when they're not dealt with biblically. The writer of Ephesians 4:3 urges Christians to be humble, gentle, and patient, "showing forbearance to one another in love, being diligent to preserve the unity of the Spirit in the bond of peace." Purpose before God this day, to work diligently to pursue peace and unity with your brothers and sisters in Christ.

"Dear Father, I want to obey Your command to strive to maintain peace with all men, as far as it depends on me."

Devotional #56

Fear Not

God instructs His children in 1 Peter 3:6 to "do what is right without being frightened by any fear." Certain fears are valid. It is legitimate, for example, not to wade very deep into the ocean for fear of drowning.

Scripture refers here, however, to fears that are groundless and irrational—fear of driving, fear of our children suddenly dying, or fear of going out in public, for example. Many Christians today are crippled by various fears and worries. They are so paralyzed by anxiety that they can't even fulfill their basic responsibilities, or accomplish their daily routine.

There is one kind of fear that is more prudent than any other. We read in Proverbs 1:7: "The fear of God is the beginning of wisdom." We can be certain that trusting in our own strength is foolishness. God, alone, is in sovereign and loving control of every detail of our lives. Even when we walk through the valley of the shadow of death, we have nothing to fear, for He promises to be with us and to comfort us.

We read a description of one way in which the Lord comforts us in 2 Timothy 1:7: "For God has not given us a spirit of timidity (fear), but of power and love and sound judgment." Our Heavenly Father is always present with His children. His powerful Holy Spirit dwells and works mightily within us. As the Psalmist asks in Psalm 56:4: "What can mere man do to us?"

Are you bound up in fear and anxiety? Obey God's Word today, and actively choose to replace your fears with thankful prayers to the Lord. In return, He will grant you His peace which surpasses human understanding, and which will guard your heart and mind. You can stand confidently on His promise in 1 John 4:18: "There is no fear in love, but perfect love casts out fear."

"Lord God, You are my Light, my Salvation, and the Strength of my life. Of whom shall I be afraid?"

Devotional #57

TGIF – Is it Biblical?

TGIF—*Thank God It's Friday*—is a rallying cry in the workplace. Most people seem to dread getting up and going to work each morning. They barely drag themselves through the workweek, doing the minimum that's required of them, and living for the upcoming weekend. But the Bible sets a higher standard for God's children. Their attitudes should reflect an understanding that there is, for the Christian, nobility in labor.

God commands Christians to be obedient to their employers. This requires a "servant's heart." He instructs us in His Word to "do our work heartily, as unto the Lord." Christian employees should have a good work ethic, and they should be enthusiastic about making other people successful in the workplace as well.

They need to learn how their employer thinks, and they should be sure they understand exactly what their employer expects of them. They may need to take notes on whatever is explained to them, and they should not hesitate to ask questions when something is unclear to them.

Faithful employees follow directions. They carry out each job exactly as they're instructed to do it. At the same time, they search for ways to be even more efficient. If their employer approves their ideas, he or she may be able to save time, money, and resources, and improve the quality of production as well.

Are you a conscientious employee who pays close attention to detail? Do you often perform your job in a way that demonstrates your commitment to do more than is required of you? Do you cheerfully include clean up as part of your routine, and do you maintain a neat work area? God's Word commands us: "Let everything be done decently and in order." Make this your goal today.

"Dear God, I believe there is dignity in labor. I desire to work diligently and enthusiastically. Teach me to submit to my employer, as unto You Lord."

Devotional #58
The Love of Money

Have you ever heard the saying, "Money is the root of all evil?" This old adage misstates the truth. The fact is that the *love* of money is *one* of many roots of evil. While God's Word certainly does not condemn the possession of money, Jesus clearly teaches in Matthew 6:24, "You cannot serve both God and mammon (riches)."

We read in the Bible that God owns the "cattle on a thousand hills." In fact, He is the Creator of the universe and He owns everything. He is a loving Heavenly Father who has entrusted to us everything that we have. We must strive to be good and faithful stewards (caretakers) of those possessions. We should, therefore, be liberal givers, dedicating all our money to God, and honoring Him with weekly tithes and offerings.

Why did Jesus tell the rich young ruler to go and sell everything he had and give his money to the poor? We know from other accounts in Scripture that Jesus did not instruct all potential converts to do that.

It was because Jesus perceived that for this particular individual, money was an idol—a god. The young man's love of money prevented him from repenting and receiving salvation. Scripture tells us he went sorrowfully away.

In Matthew 6:19-21, Jesus offers Christians specific guidelines for dealing with money: "Do not lay up for yourselves treasures on earth, where moth and rust destroy and where thieves break in and steal. But lay up for yourselves treasures in heaven, where neither moth nor rust destroys, and where thieves do not break in and steal, for where your treasure is, there your heart will be also."

"Lord, make me a faithful and generous steward. You have blessed me bountifully with all good things and I could never out-give You."

Devotional #59
Submitting to Authority

It seems that few people today want to be under anyone's authority. Children don't want their parents telling them what to do, wives refuse to "honor and obey" their husbands, and employees freely file grievances against employers. In our society, a pervasive attitude of proud independence has, for the most part, supplanted the virtue of a submissive spirit.

The writer of 1 Peter 5:5 clearly states that we should all be in submission to authority: "All of you be subject one to another, and be clothed with humility, for God resists the proud, and gives grace to the humble." All authority comes from God, but He delegates His authority to four earthly structures—the family, the church, the government, and employers. We learn in 1 Peter 2:13,14 that the purpose of authority is to punish evildoers and to praise those people who do well.

Christians find a stern warning in Romans 13:1,2: "Let every person be in subjection to the governing authorities. For there is no authority except from God, and those that exist, are established by God. Therefore, he who resists authority has opposed the ordinance of God; and they who have opposed will receive condemnation upon themselves."

The Lord expects His children to submit willingly to God-ordained authority structures within the family, the church, the government, and places of employment, with a grateful heart and a respectful attitude.

We must never, however, obey the commands of any authority that asks us to do something that would violate Scripture. In such an instance, we should appeal to our authority wisely and humbly, respectfully offering an alternative suggestion, and using the Word of God as our final authority.

"Lord, I ask You to subdue the rebellion in my heart and to use my willing submission to authority as a testimony for Your glory."

Devotional #60
A Living Sacrifice

The animal sacrifices that were made regularly in Old Testament times were done away with forever after Jesus' atoning death on the cross. He was the perfect Lamb of God, and He was the final and ultimate sacrifice for the forgiveness of our iniquities.

Today, God commands His children to be a "living sacrifice." He instructs us in Romans 12:1: "Present your bodies a living and holy sacrifice, acceptable to God, which is your spiritual service of worship."

In order to be an effective *living sacrifice,* you must give God control over the two most important areas of your life—your time and your money. A pastor friend once explained that if he had the opportunity to review a person's daily schedule and his checkbook register, he could estimate, with a fair amount of accuracy, the degree of that person's commitment to Christ.

Everyone has the same amount of time allotted to him every day. And although we all have differing amounts of money, it's a fact that almost every decision we make involves finances.

You may have heard the saying that the trouble with a living sacrifice is, it keeps crawling off the altar. Those who are the redeemed of God have been purchased with Christ's blood, and their bodies are not their own.

One Bible translation renders the second verse of Romans 12 in this way: "Do not let yourself be *squeezed* into the mold of this world." If you want to experience God's perfect will for your life, ask God to transform you by renewing your mind. Above all, understand that your chief purpose in life—the ultimate reason for which you were born—is to praise and glorify Him.

"Dear Father, I acknowledge that You are the Creator of all things and the Sovereign Ruler over all creation. Make my life a living sacrifice, acceptable in Your sight."

Resources

To order these books, visit us on the Web at:
biblicalcounseling.com

You *Are* Your Sister's Keeper (Uncomplicated Ministering, Girlfriend to Girlfriend) [$12.95]

by Dr. Debbi Dunlap

Description: Mentoring! God calls women to invest their lives in faith-cultivating relationships with other women. Yet who has time or motivation to commit to another training program? So Debbi has done the footwork to save you prep time as you minister to the complex needs women face today. Not a front-to-back read, this "cafeteria-style" book contains principles and related scriptures addressing aspects of every woman's faith journey. Whatever topic you're dealing with, you'll find a concise, substantive "jumping-off" guide in this exciting new resource. Written by an experienced pastor's wife/mother of 10, this book is a gold-mine for women dedicated to initiating meaningful faith-cultivating relationships.

A Purpose-Driven Past [$10.95]

by Dr. Don Dunlap

Description: Many Christians are confused about forgiveness--what it is and what it isn't. Oversimplification abounds! Why is it vitally important to understand how to forgive biblically? Refusing to forgive has far-reaching interpersonal consequences and also results in severe emotional and spiritual problems. When we misunderstand the forgiveness process we miss the benefits God intends us to derive from our trials and problems. Dr. Dunlap, a counselor for more than 20 years and 25,000 counseling appointments, expertly leads you through the practical insights needed to master biblical forgiveness.

Forgive and Never Forget! The Journey, Destination, and Practice of Forgiveness - Practical Workbook [$14.95]

by Dr. Don Dunlap

Description: This book contains the chapters found in "Purpose-Driven Past," and also includes study guides at the end of every few chapters. Use this workbook with small groups, or as a special emphasis study, to teach and reinforce the biblical principles of forgiveness. Refusing to forgive has far-reaching interpersonal consequences, and also results in severe emotional and spiritual problems. When we misunderstand the forgiveness process we miss the benefits God intends us to derive from our trials and problems. Dr. Dunlap, a counselor for more than 20 years and

25,000 counseling appointments, expertly leads you through the practical insights needed to master biblical forgiveness.

Straighten Up and Fly Right Parents! (Getting Spiritual Backbone to Discipline Your Kids) [$8.95]

By Drs. Don and Debbi Dunlap

Description: "You have to the count of three to obey me!" Do those words sound familiar? How about, "Do as I say, not as I do!" Or that time-honored threat, "You're grounded!" Interested in finding out why all these disciplinary techniques are ineffective? The authors have ten children and more parenting experience than they bargained for! If you're held hostage by disrespectful, unruly kids, this little power-packed book could rescue you! Don, an experienced and trusted family counselor, and Debbi, a women's conference leader, will help you understand the biblical principles of child discipline.

Help! I Married FrankenSpouse (Fixing Your Marriage Before It Becomes a Horror Story) [$8.95]

By Drs. Don and Debbi Dunlap

Description: After a few years (or less!) of marriage, lots of husbands and wives feel they're not married to the same person they exchanged wedding vows with. The authors, respected and experienced family counselors, help you unravel this mystery and make your way back to a fulfilling marriage relationship. Spouse "Offense" checklists, and several chapters on dealing with the devastating effects of adultery make this little book an absolute must-buy!

Stop Acting Like a Baby! (Dealing with Anger—God's Way) [$8.95]

By Drs. Don and Debbi Dunlap

Description: Seems no matter where we go these days, we usually end up witnessing an angry shouting match, or hearing foul, uncensored language anytime someone is the least bit provoked. It's suddenly OK for adults to pitch angry fits (like grown-up babies) to get their anger out, if that's what works for them. But the truth hasn't changed: unbridled anger is deadly when it comes to maintaining solid, meaningful, nurturing relationships. This book offers you an effective, biblical plan to deal with anger in a way that enhances relationships, and enlarges the scope of your Christian testimony.

About the Authors

Don Dunlap, former Senior Editor for Counseling and feature writer on counseling and family for the Christianity.com Network, has conducted over 25,000 counseling appointments during his ministerial career. A leading Pastoral Counselor and pioneer in the placement of Pastoral Counselors in the offices of Christian physicians, Don is founder and director of Family Physician Partners, and has established offices in South Carolina, North Carolina, Alabama, Georgia, and Florida.

As the Director of Family Counseling Ministries, with headquarters in Jacksonville, Florida, Don conducts Family Life Conferences, Parent Training Seminars, and Marriage Enrichment Retreats.

Don has a degree in Child Development from Florida State University, and a Master's Degree in Education and Theology (specializing in Marriage and Family Counseling) from Southwestern Baptist Theological Seminary. He holds a Doctor of Ministry degree from Luther Rice Seminary. His counseling practice includes adults, children, and families in crisis. Don also provides telephone counseling for individuals who are unable to meet face-to-face with a competent, Bible-based counselor.

Don and Debbi have been married since 1976, and they are the parents of ten children. Debbi traveled for several years as a child performer with the Grand Ol' Opry, appearing with such stars as Johnny Cash, June Carter, Jim Reeves, and Marty Robbins. While a student at Florida State University, Debbi served on youth staff at First Baptist Church, Tallahassee. She attended Southern Seminary in Louisville, Kentucky, and Southwestern Seminary in Fort Worth, Texas, and has a Master's degree in Counseling. She also holds a Doctor of Practical Theology and Administration degree from Master's School of Divinity.

For many years, Debbi has home-schooled their ten children. She also serves as a speaker for women's conferences and retreats. Don and Debbi have authored several books, and have written numerous articles related to marriage and family. You can contact them at their website, www.biblicalcounseling.com.